ALWAYS OBEDIENT

ALWAYS OBEDIENT

*Essays on the Teachings of
Dr. Klaas Schilder*

EDITED BY

J. Geertsema

P&R
PUBLISHING
P.O. BOX 817 • PHILLIPSBURG • NEW JERSEY 08865-0817

Printed in the United States of America
Co-published in Canada by Inheritance Publications, Box 154, Neerlandia, AB.

Library of Congress Cataloging-in-Publication Data

Always obedient : essays on the teaching of Dr. Klaas Schilder / edited by
    J. Geertsema.
            p.   cm.
    Includes bibliographical references and index.
    ISBN 0-87552-239-4 (pbk.)
    1. Schilder, K. (Klaas), 1890–1952—Contributions in theology.
  I. Geertsema, J. (Jacob), 1935–
BX9479.S35.A48   1995
230—dc20   95-44258

CONTENTS

FOREWORD

J. Geertsema

It is a great joy to present this book about Dr. Klaas Schilder (1890–1952). This joy comes from the fact that what Schilder taught as the doctrines of God's covenant Word spoken to and written down for His people arouses a profound delight in the heart of the believer. In these teachings the rich treasures of the Scripture are painted before our eyes with the clear strokes of the fine pen of a skilled scribe trained for the kingdom of heaven. As a faithful householder, he brought out of his treasure new and old for the household of God (Matt. 13:52). It was a delight for those who listened to this servant of God and of His church to enjoy the food of God's Word as he placed it before them; this very same delight can be the portion of those who enjoy these treasures today.

The idea for this book was conceived in the spring of 1990. The senate of the theological college of the Canadian Reformed Churches in Hamilton decided that also in Canada attention should be drawn to the fact that a century ago Klaas Schilder was born. The reason is the important role that Schilder played in the history of the Reformed Churches (Liberated) in the Netherlands and his significance for their sister churches on other continents. Outside these Reformed churches Schilder is relatively unknown. It is the purpose of this publication to present Schilder and his teachings to readers in the English-speaking world, and it is our conviction that his insight into the Scriptures and his faithful adherence to the Reformed confessions, whereby he enriched the lives of so many believers, should not be lost but should continue to instruct and guide us. It was Schilder who once said, "It is a delight to be Reformed."

First the senate organized three evening lectures for the general public in November of the commemoration year, 1990. In the first evening Dr. J. De Jong addressed the audience concerning Schilder's teaching on God's revelation (a specific aspect of this teaching, namely God's accommodation, had been the topic of Dr. De Jong's doctoral dissertation); in the second evening Dr. N. H. Gootjes spoke on Schilder's view of "Christ and culture"; and in the third evening an overview of Schilder's life and work was presented by Dr. J. Faber.

At a later stage, when discussing the publication of these three addresses, the senate decided to add a few chapters dealing with other important aspects of Schilder's teachings. Accordingly, Dr. S. A. Strauss, professor of dogmatics at the University of Orange Free State, Bloemfontein, South Africa, provided a contribution about Schilder's teaching on the covenant. Dr. Strauss had written a doctoral dissertation on this subject. J. M. Batteau, currently minister of God's Word in the Reformed Church (Liberated) in Wageningen, the Netherlands, had studied Schilder's teaching on the church, and he contributed an article on this topic. Prof. J. Kamphuis of the Theological University of the Reformed Churches (Liberated) in Kampen, the Netherlands, had written a paper on Schilder's book *Wat is de Hemel?* (What Is Heaven?). This paper was originally one of twenty addresses on Schilder's life and ideas presented at a symposium at the Free University of Amsterdam on April 6, 1990, to commemorate the birth of Schilder a century earlier. These addresses were published in *Geen Duimbreed!*[1] We thank both J. Kamphuis, the author, and Ten Have, the publisher, for permission to print this article in our book. D. W. Cowart, at the time of our request a student in Kampen, translated the Dutch article and supplied references to the English translation of *Wat is de Hemel?* by M. M. Schooland. We express our gratitude to him for his assistance. We also thank Dr. R. Faber for his help in preparing the manuscript of this present book for publication.

Since this book contains six essays about the teachings of one man, some repetition could not be avoided. Such repetition shows the extent to which Schilder's teachings regarding different aspects of biblical doctrine are linked together and form a unity.

There is a certain logic to the order in which the six contributions are presented here. The book begins with the contribution of Dr. J. Faber, since it presents an overview of Schilder's life and work. It will enable the reader to place the other contributions in the context of Schilder's life and struggle for the Lord Jesus Christ and for His church, which was at the same time a fight for the authority of God's Word.

Schilder saw his life and work very much as a matter of obedient covenant service. The covenant of God with His people, as it is revealed in Scripture and as it functioned throughout biblical history, had an important, even a dominant place in Schilder's theological thinking. However, it was not just a theological theory for him. God's covenant in Christ with its promises and obligations dominated just as much his life, work, and actions. Schilder lived by God's promises. He sought to obey God's revealed will in the concrete social, political, and ecclesiastical situations in his life, aiming to lead others along the same way of faith in faithfulness to the Lord and His Word. Since God's covenant had such a primary place in Schilder's life and thought, Dr. Strauss's contribution forms chapter 2.

Schilder not only emphasized the character of the covenant as a living relationship between God and His people, but he also stressed its historical framework and evolvement. Schilder saw all history, including the history of the covenant, as a unity, because all history is the work of the triune God Himself. In the beginning the Father created heaven and earth through His Son in cooperation with the Holy Spirit, making man after His image to be His child and viceroy on earth. As a consequence of man's fall into sin, God worked redemption through the death and resurrection of His incarnate Son, anointed with the Holy Spirit for this task, when the time for it in the history of the covenant had fully come. And the same God, through His exalted Son, guides the history of the covenant to its consummation in "these last days," which are characterized as the dispensation of the Holy Spirit, who gathers the church of Christ out of all the nations and brings her to the coming glory of the New Jerusalem.

The unity of history, including the history of the covenant, means the unity of Creation and redemption. Schilder stressed this unity. God's covenant with man did not begin after the fall into sin. He established it as the "so-called covenant of works" (better is probably the name "covenant of favor")[2] with Adam and Eve in Paradise, promising to be their God and Father and to lead them to eternal life in the way of obedient faith. After the fall into sin, God did not abolish His creation, but in His covenant, which became a covenant of grace in Christ, He maintained what He had created. Christ is the Redeemer not just of the soul but of God's whole creation. Through Him God reconciled to Himself all things both in heaven and on earth (Col. 1:20). Therefore, Christ is already in principle the Redeemer for God's children in all aspects of created life here on this earth. Christ redeems those who believe in Him from unbelief and sin, making them live again for God, for instance, in their marriages and in their family life, in their labor relations and in their daily work (Col. 3:18–4:1).

That Christ's work of redemption applies to the marriages of believers is evident from other texts, too. God created male and female and instituted marriage with its ordinance that a man shall leave his father and mother and cleave to her who has legally become his wife and that the two shall become one flesh. This command of Genesis 2:24 is fully in force after the fall into sin, as Christ in Matthew 19:5 and Paul in Ephesians 5:31 show. In spite of our sinful condition, God keeps marriage as He had instituted it. Sin distorts and breaks down what God has created, but Christ, in His redemption, brings us back to God's laws that were in effect from the beginning.

This example of marriage as part of daily life can be used to show that Schilder was correct, scripturally, when he developed his teaching regarding our "cultural mandate." This is the mandate—the daily task—that Adam and Eve, and with them mankind, received from God in the Garden of Eden: to cultivate and guard the earth. Schilder would also call this cultural mandate an "office." In our daily task we are God's appointed office-bearers. This mandate or office is related to man's creation after God's image. Therefore, it is the office of king, priest, and prophet. Adam's and Eve's cultivating and guarding of the Garden of Eden and our daily task is our office of having royal dominion on earth, which office is to be executed for God with priestly dedication and in prophetic wisdom within the framework of God's covenant of favor with mankind.

According to Schilder, this calling for man to do his daily work on God's earth for God as His office-bearers remains the same after the fall into sin. We are to fulfill our daily task on earth, whatever it is, in the service of God, in light of both the Paradise mandate (Creation) and the restoration by Christ of what God created (redemption). Slaves in Colossae heard the gospel of redemption through Christ in their daily slave work. They could do that work for the Lord Jesus Christ in faith, being renewed in true knowledge after the image of God (Col. 3:10). This mandate or office from the beginning, maintained after the Fall and restored in Christ, is the topic of the third contribution, N. H. Gootjes's essay on Schilder's teaching regarding Christ and culture.

The fourth essay, by J. M. Batteau, deals with Schilder's views on the church. Schilder's understanding of what Scripture teaches about the covenant, with its two parts, promise and obligation, influenced his thoughts and actions regarding the church. According to Schilder, we should not define the church as the static total number of all the elect, the church as it will be on the new earth. The church is first of all the result of the gathering activity of Christ. In an ongoing process, He gathers, defends, and preserves His church, chosen to everlasting life, by His Spirit and Word. The church may be called the people of the new covenant. This means, among other things, that the ongoing gathering activity of Christ can be seen as fulfillment of God's promise. In response to this promise, believers now are to gather with Christ in obedience to the revealed will of God. This is our covenant obligation. Schilder wanted to maintain the norm of God's Word for the true church of Christ and for individual obedient church membership as expressed in the Reformed confessions. Thus, also in Schilder's writing about the church we find the theme "all or nothing," as this theme characterized his understanding and teaching of the covenant. We find it also in Schilder's emphatic use of the biblical notion and confessional terminology of "true" and "false" in connection with the church.

Recent criticism of Schilder's teaching on the church states that he did not reckon sufficiently with the brokenness of life and sinful human reality. However, it would be better to say that Schilder was fully aware of the sinful reality and the brokenness of life, also as this becomes manifest in the church in the separation of brothers and sisters into different denominations. In this awareness he fought against pious reasons for acceptance of the sinful reality of the brokenness of the church. Schilder had a keen eye for the danger that acceptance of the status quo interferes with humble and simple covenantal obedience to the revealed will of God. Schilder's aim in his polemics about the church was to open the eyes of God's people to the promises and the demands of God's covenant Word and to call them to join in obedience to God's Word on the points of being the church and of church membership. It is not unimaginable that those who criticize Schilder with the accusation that he did not reckon with the sinful reality of life in fact promote and strengthen the passive acceptance of this sinful situation and in this way obstruct and undermine the biblical obedience of faith to what is written, as well as the brotherly faithfulness entailed in "maintaining the unity of the Church."[3]

Moving from the office in the beginning of the covenant's history—the cultural mandate—we come via Christ's church-gathering work to the consummation of the covenant, a topic treated by Professor J. Kamphuis. For Schilder heaven is not just "a static immovable sphere," but it is "taken up in the framework of history." God guides heaven and earth through the one history of the covenant. He comes from the beginning in Creation to the fulfillment of His purpose, that is, to the covenant of glory, when Christ returns and God will be with His people and they will be with Him forever in everlasting light. Kamphuis sounds a note of criticism when he stresses that the consummation, too, will not mean a static immovable sphere but an eternal, active reign with Christ to the glory of God. In the consummation, on the new earth, when the New Jerusalem has come down to the earth, man's office, his cultural mandate instituted from the beginning, will find its fulfillment. The believers, those whom the Father gave to His Son and for whom the Son died and rose, will reign on earth with Christ as priestly kings, crowned with glory and honor.[4]

Schilder was a polemical author. The different contributions in this volume show this. He opposed scholastic distinctions in the theological system of Kuyper and his followers. He rejected the dialectical theology of Karl Barth. He also fought against the philosophy of national socialism and against all forms of humanism. In this spiritual warfare Schilder's weapon was the revelation of God. God's Word was his basis. Without compromise he accepted and defended it as infallible and inerrant, as the sole basis and norm for faith and life in the covenant with God. Instructed as he was by Scripture, Schilder instructed others, stressing in particular the biblical, Reformed doctrines of the covenant, of the church, and of the office (i.e., man's cultural mandate, his daily task, restored by Christ as the great Office-bearer, our great King, Priest, and Prophet).

The revelation of God as Schilder's basis is the subject of Dr. De Jong's contribution. Over against Karl Barth and his followers, Schilder maintained that the Bible *is* God's Word. And over against Kuyper and his followers, he maintained that the Word of God is the means through which God works faith, regeneration, and conversion. Thus, with God's revelation as the basis for everything, this introduction to the teachings of Schilder is rounded off.

If, after having read this study of Schilder, one should wish to characterize the man and his work in a few words, one could quote the title of the book in which Professor Kamphuis's contribution first appeared, "Not even an inch!"

The expression "not even an inch" originated with Abraham Kuyper. With it he expressed the kingship of Christ over all aspects or spheres of life. He wrote, "There is not a square inch within the domain of our human life of which the Christ, who is the Sovereign over all, does not say, 'Mine'."[5] Kuyper meant hereby that Christ must be acknowledged as King in every part of life. This includes the political part. Schilder used this title in 1936 for a brochure in which he showed that a Christian should not be a member of a national socialist political party. When national socialists of Hitler's Germany occupied the Netherlands in May 1940, Schilder used "his" weekly *De Reformatie* to continue to wage spiritual warfare against the movement of national socialism. He did not budge "even an inch," though it cost him imprisonment and persecution. It was for him simply a matter of covenant obedience to the Lord and of covenant faithfulness to one's neighbor, in particular to God's people.

This same obedience to God and God's Word guided Schilder

in the controversy involving the Reformed Churches during the Second World War. When the general synods in the forties made binding doctrinal decisions that Schilder was convinced were in conflict with both Scripture and confession, and when these synods, in conflict with the adopted Church Order, disciplined and deposed Schilder and many other dissenting office bearers, he saw the way of liberating himself from such incorrect pronouncements and unjustified actions as the way of obedience to God's Word and as faithfulness to the ecclesiastical agreements.

Schilder opposed that form of Christianity which can speak piously but which refuses to obey God's Word in the Scriptures. Not even an inch, all or nothing—that is Schilder. Humble obedience in faith to God's revealed Word was what characterized him. It is our prayer and hope that God will bless the publication of this book so that Schilder's insight into the teachings of God's Word as confessed in the Reformed standards may continue to bring us to the conclusion that "it is a delight to be Reformed." It is a delight to live obediently by God's revelation in Christ Jesus, our Lord and Savior.

Notes

1. J. de Bruijn and G. Harinck, eds., *Geen Duimbreed! Facetten van Leven en Werk van Prof. Dr. K. Schilder 1890–1952* (Not Even an Inch! Aspects of Prof. Dr. K. Schilder's Life and Work) (Baarn: Ten Have, 1990).
2. Schilder did not like the phrase *covenant of works.* In fact, he often placed the word *so-called* in front of the term. The phrase can give the impression that in this covenant man has to obtain eternal life by his good works. Schilder strongly asserted that man can never earn anything with God, not even in the "state of righteousness," since whatever man can do he does only because it is given him by God. Man cannot present to God anything that is truly all his own. In connection with this covenant Schilder spoke about God's favor (*gunst*), even though he had difficulty using the expression "covenant of favor," as S. A. Strauss observes in S. A. Strauss, *Alles of Niks. K. Schilder Oor die Verbond* (All or Nothing. K. Schilder on the Covenant), diss. (Bloemfontein, South Africa: Patmos, 1986), 83, and as Schilder himself taught in K. Schilder, *Capita Selecta I* (Lecture notes) (Kampen: Theological University, 1949), 45–46; see also K. Schilder, *Heidelbergsche Catechismus,* 4 vols. (Goes: Oosterbaan & Le Cointre, 1947–51), 1:392.
3. Article 28 of the Belgic Confession, in *Book of Praise of the Canadian Reformed Churches* (Winnipeg: Premier, 1984), 462.
4. The promise of Ps. 8, that man is to have dominion, is based upon God's cre-

ation of man in His own image and is explained in the light of Christ in Heb. 2:5–9. Christ, through His satisfying suffering, leads believers to this glorious fulfillment.

5. The quotation is taken from A. Kuyper, *Souvereiniteit in Eigen Kring. Rede ter Inwijding van de Vrije Universiteit* (Sphere Sovereignty. Address at the Institution of the Free University [October 20, 1880]) (Kampen: Kok, 1930), 32.

1

KLAAS SCHILDER'S LIFE AND WORK

J. Faber

This chapter is divided into three parts: (1) Klaas Schilder's life, (2) his publications, and (3) his significance.

Schilder's Life

Klaas Schilder was born on December 19, 1890, in Kampen, the Netherlands. He attended the Reformed grammar school and theological seminary there and became a minister of the Word at Ambt-Vollenhove in June of 1914. Later he served the Reformed churches of Vlaardingen, Gorinchem, Delft, Oegstgeest, and Rotterdam-Delfshaven. While at Rotterdam-Delfshaven he was given leave to continue his studies at the Friedrich Alexander University in Erlangen, Germany. There he heard in particular the philosophy lectures of his promoter, Professor E. Herrigel. Schilder obtained his degree at Erlangen *summa cum laude* with a dissertation on the history of the paradox concept, paying special attention to the period after the Danish philosopher S. Kierkegaard and comparing this concept to what Calvin had written about God's revelation.

In 1933 the Synod of Middelburg unanimously appointed him

professor of dogmatics at the theological seminary in Kampen. His lectures were interrupted by trips to the United States in 1939 and 1947. During the war his teaching was stopped by the Germans, first only briefly and later for a longer period. Schilder was arrested already in August of 1940 by the German security police (SD) because of the principled and courageous stand taken in his writings in "his" weekly magazine *De Reformatie*. He was imprisoned in Arnhem until December of 1940. He was then ordered to refrain from publishing. Later he had to go into hiding again, from July of 1942 until August of 1944.

Schilder, together with his retired colleague Dr. S. Greijdanus, was suspended from office as professor and minister by the Synod of Utrecht on March 23, 1944, and deposed on August 3, 1944, because he opposed the doctrinal statements of 1942 (concerning covenant and baptism, presumed regeneration, and "common grace") and because he opposed the hierarchical actions of the synods held in 1939–43 and 1943–45. This hierarchy was evident in the high-handed self-continuation of the Synod of Sneek-Utrecht from 1939 onwards, which Schilder correctly saw to be in conflict with article 50 of the Church Order.[1]

In a meeting of aggrieved and concerned church members held on August 11, 1944, in the Lutheran church at The Hague, Klaas Schilder read the Declaration of Liberation or Return, which he had prepared.[2]

Let me add a personal note. After the meeting in The Hague on this memorable day, the students of the theological seminary in Kampen who were present thronged around Schilder—he was an honorary member of their student body—and met with him in a separate room. There we were, dozens of theology students. The majority of the Kampen students did not accept the disciplinary measures against their esteemed professors Greijdanus and Schilder. Now Schilder could easily have abused the respect and enthusiasm of his students. But he made a speech that at least to me is unforgettable. "Listen," he said, "I am nothing but a deposed professor." Only the church at Bergschenhoek had been placed outside the confederation of the Reformed Churches, and that church would call candidate H. J. Schilder, who had not been admitted to the ministry in the Reformed Churches.

Schilder told us frankly, "I do not promise you anything." And in the same manner in which Dr. Greijdanus had urged us to make the decision to sign the Declaration of Liberation *only in faith,* Schilder said, "We are like Abraham; we are called to a place that we do not know. We have to go out in *faith.*" At the meeting of August 11, 1944, in The Hague Schilder spoke and acted as a reformer of God's church. He was blind to the future and obedient to God's demand in the present.

Schilder remained as a professor in the service of the Reformed Churches, since the Liberated Churches immediately asked him, as well as Professor Greijdanus and Dr. R. J. Dam, to continue training students for the ministry.

Dr. Dam was executed by German soldiers in 1945. But after the war, in the fall of the same year, Drs. Greijdanus and Schilder resumed their teaching in an old decrepit YMCA building on the Oudestraat in Kampen, just on the other side of our former seminary building. It was primitive. A bedroom washstand functioned as the lectern for our two professors. The two gave all the lectures: the New Testament professor also taught Old Testament exegesis, and Schilder was not only our teacher in dogmatology, but also in church history. Moreover, he conducted our sermon sessions in an especially unforgettable manner. In the following year, 1946, the provisional Synod of Enschede appointed three new professors: Benne Holwerda, Pieter Deddens, and Cornelis Veenhof. How elated Schilder was when this synod also finally recognized the right of the Theological Seminary to grant the degree of doctor of theology, and how joyous was the reception that the students in Kampen gave him after his return from the Synod of Enschede!

Schilder had resumed not only his lectures, especially those in dogmatics on the doctrine of God, but also his work as editor in chief of *De Reformatie.* He worked strenuously and untiringly, often into the wee hours of the morning. Once when we met him early in the morning on his way to the mailbox, we said, "You are early, Professor." The answer was "I am a little bit late, *amici!*" His rumpled clothes and his sometimes grumpy mood during the first morning hour of his lectures made it clear to us that our professor had again not slept. Schilder worked relentlessly to defend the Liberated Churches against attacks from the outside and from the inside. Against upcoming difficulties in these churches he did what he could to keep them together in the unity of true faith.

On March 23, 1952, he died, rather unexpectedly for the outsider, due to a heart failure, precisely eight years to the day after his suspension from office as minister of the Word and professor of dogmatics. In childlike faith he had confided to his colleague Deddens, "It is well with me, I go to Jesus."[3]

Schilder's Publications

Besides teaching, Schilder devoted himself to publishing, the result of which has been summed up in an extensive forty-five-page small-print bibliography, published in the 1953 *Almanak* of Kampen's student society *Fides Quadrat Intellectum*.

Schilder's work can be classified into three periods: 1920–30, 1930–40, and 1944–52.

1920–30

It was during the period from 1920 to 1930 that Schilder made his mark. Kuyper and Bavinck had passed away in 1920. After that, on the one hand a number of slavish followers of Kuyper tried to establish themselves, while on the other hand a "movement of the younger generation" developed. This latter movement began to distance itself from the Reformed confessions in many respects and culminated in the establishment of the Gereformeerde Kerken in Hersteld Verband (Reformed Churches in Restored Federation), led by Dr. J. G. Geelkerken and the Rev. J. J. Buskes. After the Second World War, these churches ended up in the Dutch Reformed Church. It was also during these years that Karl Barth and Emil Brunner with their so-called dialectical theology made great gains.

Schilder interacted with these movements in numerous articles in church magazines and in *De Reformatie*. Through his many articles he became an important spokesman within the Reformed Churches. Moreover, Schilder began to publish a number of books. A lecture about hell grew into a book called *Wat is de Hel?* (What Is Hell?) in

1919. He placed the terrible reality of hell against the background of God's dealings with responsible man. His book *Kerktaal en Leven* (Church Language and Life), published in 1923, was an attack against mystical old-fashioned church language. Also in 1923 he published two collections of articles, *Licht in den Rook* (Light Through the Smoke), in which he attempted to show the relevance of texts from the Bible to the problems of the day. Similarly, he connected the book of Revelation with social and economic realities in *De Openbaring van Johannes en het Sociale Leven* (The Revelation to John and Life in Society). When J. G. Geelkerken denied the historical reality of parts of the Paradise narrative in Genesis 3 and was judged to be wrong by the Synod of Assen of the Reformed Churches in 1926, Schilder wrote against him, defending the doctrinal judgment of this synod in the brochure *Hoornstoot tegen Assen?* (Horn-butting Against Assen?).

At the same time collections of essays came off the press. *Bij Dichters en Schriftgeleerden* (Among Poets and Scribes, 1927) contains an essay on the paradox in religion. In this preparatory work for his thesis Schilder defended the Reformed confessions regarding the clarity or perspicuity of God's revelation in Holy Scripture. He defended these confessions against dialectical theologians like K. Barth and T. L. Haitjema. The incarnate Word did not merely twinkle among us, but it *dwelt* among us. Schilder appealed to Deuteronomy 30 and Romans 10: the Word is near you! His second large work, *Tusschen "Ja" en "Neen"* (Between Yes and No, 1929), has an essay about Calvin and the paradox of faith, and it offers an attack on the advancing dialectical theology as introduced by Professor Haitjema of the State University of Groningen.

In viewing this first period, 1920–30, we observe that Schilder took stands on all issues in defense of the truth of God. He threw himself into the thick of the struggle of the spirits; he attacked the late-flowering "ethical theology" and condemned the mysticism in Reformed circles, but he resisted in particular the ideas of Karl Barth, whose unscriptural, false-philosophical designs Schilder was among the first to recognize.

During these first ten years of publishing, Schilder also produced a forceful impulse for renewed and positive research of Holy

Scripture. Utilizing the work of Reformed exegetes such as C. Van
Gelderen, M. Noordtzij, and F. W. Grosheide and S. Greijdanus (in
the series *Korte Verklaring* [Brief Explanations]), as well as the New
Testament commentaries published by Van Bottenburg, Schilder
unfolded and defended the redemptive-historical and revelation-
historical approach to preaching.[4] Having been blessed with great gifts
for synthesis and imaginative association, Schilder showed the co-
herence and connections in Holy Scripture. His work caused the formation of a school of mostly young Reformed ministers and led to
the renewal of the preaching of the Word in an inspiring manner. This
labor reached a summit in 1930 with the publication of *Christus in
Zijn Lijden* (Christ in His Suffering), a trilogy that was ably translated
into English.[5] In poetic, at times abundant language, this work accented the threefold office of the Christ, who is prophet, priest, and
king. Because it combined Reformed exegesis and Reformed dogmatics, this work was no doubt of great significance. The language
that Schilder used might now be considered somewhat old-fashioned,
and one might receive the impression that Schilder's penchant to syn-
thesize sometimes led him to a somewhat forced exegesis. Yet even
today this trilogy on Christ's *passio magna* (intense suffering) will
bring believers to a deeper appreciation of the inscrutable greatness
of the suffering of Christ, and in particular to adoration of the Messiah
Jesus.

1930–40

The publication of *Christus in Zijn Lijden* in 1930 marks the transi-
tion to the second period in Schilder's publications, the period from
1930 to 1940. To Schilder's work on the doctrine of Christ belongs a
well-known essay, *Jezus Christus en het Cultuurleven* (Jesus Christ
and Cultural Life). Its second edition, prepared during Schilder's jour-
ney in 1947 to the United States, bears another title, *Christus en Cultuur* (Christ and Culture).[6] For those who wish to acquaint themselves
with Schilder, this book is an excellent introduction. It develops the
idea of the cultural mandate and places the office of the Christ and the
Christian foremost, in accordance with Lord's Day 12 of the Heidelberg Catechism.

In the overview of Schilder's life we mentioned his dissertation, *Zur Begriffsgeschichte des "Paradoxon"* (The History of the Concept of the "Paradoxon," 1933). This work reveals the philosophical schooling of the author. In keeping with his earlier studies (those of 1927 and 1929), Schilder devoted special attention to Søren Kierkegaard and Karl Barth. Over against irrationalism, Schilder maintained that although God does remove our *sins* of thought, he does not put aside His *laws* of thought.

The dissertation concluded with a review of what Calvin said about God's manner of speaking to man. With Calvin, Schilder maintained the traditional Reformed position that God's speaking in Scripture is never exhaustive yet indeed always pure and true. God's speaking to us is accommodating: in His revelation God adapts Himself to our comprehension. Schilder's thesis received renewed attention through the dissertation of H. M. Kuitert at the Free University of Amsterdam, *De Mensvormigheid Gods* (The Anthropomorphic Nature of God), which also dealt with the related topic of anthropomorphism in Scripture. I believe that in his criticism of Schilder, Dr. Kuitert reveals that he has read him inaccurately.[7] The same topic of God's accommodation was also the subject of the dissertation of J. De Jong.[8]

In January of 1934, Schilder took the chair of dogmatics at the Theological Seminary in Kampen with a speech in which he once more took issue with dialectical theology and existentialist philosophy and placed over against them faith-based obedience to the Scriptures.

Though Schilder did not publish this inaugural lecture, parts of its contents found their way into the extensive footnotes that he included in his commemorative speech of 1934, *De Dogmatische Beteekenis der Afscheiding Ook Voor Onzen Tijd* (The Dogmatic Significance of the Secession Also for Our Time).[9]

This speech shows how the Secession stood for the Canons of Dort. These Canons of Dort uphold the confession of the almighty, sovereign grace of God, which is present in history and works in history. God pronounces His "no" to sin, not to history. In his day and age Schilder saw Dort as opposing the theology of Karl Barth. He said,

> Whoever does not accept the presuppositions of Dort is fur-
> ther removed from Dort than the most convinced liberal of
> 1834, . . . but whoever accepts them, with him we are willing
> to dwell together. With him we know ourselves together to be
> bearers of the faith of the church, good patriots, children of
> the Reformation, included in the ecumenical Christianity.[10]

The same genuine, Reformed-ecumenical tone we hear also in
the beautiful brochure *"Ons Aller Moeder"—Anno Domini 1935* (The
Mother of Us All—Anno Domini 1935). This has been called "perhaps the most beautiful and pious polemic about the church ever written in the Dutch language."[11] Schilder concludes his emotional call to
the Dutch Reformed Church with the penetrating question,

> What do we, in the year of our *Lord* Jesus Christ, do for Him
> who dwells in heaven and governs from there? Moreover,
> what do we do for the hierarchy of heaven and for "the mother
> of us all"? . . . Now then, thus says that revealed Word: re-
> pent, and do it straightway, and do it in covenantal obedi-
> ence. Anno Domini 1935,—Nothing is impossible with God.[12]

In my opinion, this brochure remains valid against all sanctimonious
disobedience of churches, as well as against all sanctimonious sectarianism—which also is disobedience to the living God, who in Christ
proceeds with His church-gathering work.

Schilder, who during his time in Germany (1933) had been confronted with the grim face of national socialism, took up the fight
against the National Socialist Movement in the Netherlands in faith
and with vigor. He pointed out its philosophical background. He knew
Hegel, Wagner, and Nietzsche, and he saw through Rosenberg and
his myth of the twentieth century. The title and contents of his brochure *Geen Duimbreed!* (Not Even an Inch!) of 1936,[13] as well as his
advice to the 1936 Synod of Amsterdam in his opposition to H. H.
Kuyper, showed him to be a faithful adherent to the principles of the
Anti-Revolutionary Party, established by Abraham Kuyper.

In the meantime students had arranged the publication of
Schilder's lecture notes. Exhaustively and extensively he dealt with

introductory questions of theology, with ethics, and, in dogmatics, especially with the doctrine about God. Parallel with this, he presented topical lectures on the church and on the covenant of God in the Reformed confessions. After the publication of a book on this topic, the doctrine of the covenant again received all of Schilder's attention in a series of ten articles.[14] In opposition to scholastic Kuyperianism, Schilder returned to the Reformed theologians of the sixteenth century. Similarly in later years, after the Second World War, Schilder went still further back in his dogmatic studies, namely to the so-called church fathers.

In his book *Wat is de Hemel?* (What Is Heaven?) Schilder had already corrected Abraham Kuyper's views on "common grace."[15] During the press debate of the 1930s his criticism sharpened, as did the opposition from the side of those who loathed any criticism of Kuyper. This led to insinuations that reached their low point at the 1936 Synod of Amsterdam and in Dr. V. Hepp's series of booklets *Dreigende Deformatie* (Impending Deformation).[16]

There was also a debate in the press about Kuyper's doctrine of the pluriformity of the church in which Schilder, with an eye for covenantal obedience and the call to true church unity, placed all emphasis on the confessional distinction of true and false churches. In the midst of these polemics war broke out and the Germans overran the Netherlands.

It is in times like these that both moral weakness and ethical strength are revealed. Of the latter Schilder's articles bore witness: "Leave your hiding-place, don your uniform!" With a strong appeal to international law Schilder fought the battle for spiritual freedom. At the same time he used the weapon of his sharp pen and persisted tirelessly in the struggle against the anti-Christian ideology of national socialism.

In August of 1940 Schilder wrote,

> *Authority* and *power*, fortunately, remain two things. Eventually the antichrist shall keep *the latter* and the church *the former*. And after that the day of the great harvest comes. Come, Lord of the harvest, yes come quickly, come over the [English] Channel and over the Brenner Pass, come via Mal-

ta and Japan, yes, come from the ends of the earth, and bring
along your pruning-knife, and be merciful to your people; it
is well authorized, but only through Thee, through Thee alone,
at Thy eternal good pleasure.[17]

Then he was arrested. The book *Bezet Bezit* (Occupied Possession)
still makes fascinating reading, and it remains a mystery that the official recognition of Schilder's Christian resistance against national
socialism came many years after the war, in 1982.[18]

Similarly incomprehensible is the fact that in the middle of this
war, under the leadership of Dr. G. C. Berkouwer, who later regretted
his action, Schilder was suspended, yes, deposed from his office. The
dogmatician of Kampen had loved the Reformed Churches with his
whole heart and had used his great mental faculties to defend these
churches and their confessions against attacks from without and deformation from within. But in the dark year of 1944, a general synod
of these churches dismissed him as professor and as minister of the
Word while he was hiding from the Germans.

The liberation of the Netherlands and the liberation within the
Reformed Churches was the beginning of the third and last period of
his life and work.

1944–52

The last period is formed by Schilder's final eight years (1944–52).
In these years he wrote numerous articles and some brochures concerning the struggle for the liberation of the churches, the struggle
against the new hierarchical church polity and against the ecclesiastical binding to suprascriptural doctrines imposed by the synods of
1939–42 and 1943–45.

In the brochure *Looze Kalk* (Untempered Mortar),[19] Schilder
opposed the theory of Dr. J. Ridderbos that regarded God's covenant
as established through and in regeneration. Schilder did not accept a
mutual identification of covenant and election, and he rose to defend
the unique character of God's promising Word. We are not allowed
to treat the promise as though it were a prediction about the elect.
God's promise comes to all the children of His covenant indiscrimi-

nately and seriously. The promise of God is accompanied by the command to repent and believe. Untiringly Schilder conducted the defense of the right, indeed, the duty, of believers to liberate themselves from wrong theological opinions imposed upon them and to liberate themselves from unlawful church discipline. He devoted much precious time and energy to a variety of minor matters, including those relating to differences that arose within the Liberated Churches themselves.

Yet during the same period he prepared new editions of several books (for example, vols. 1 and 2 of *Christus in Zijn Lijden*) and also continued his commentary on the Heidelberg Catechism. He had already started this commentary before the war in the form of a weekly insert in *De Reformatie*, but he rewrote the first part and continued after the war. The four monumental volumes deal with Lord's Days 1–10. Although, because of Schilder's death, this work remained incomplete, it is his dogmatic masterpiece. It embodies Schilder's lectures and demonstrates his wide reading, not only in the theology dating from the time of the Reformation, but also in the Greek and Latin church fathers. In his *Heidelbergsche Catechismus* the fight against dialectical theology continued, for example, in a searching review of Barth's speculation concerning God's act of creation. Barth wrote about the concept of *das Nichtige* (Nothingness) and made a distinction between the work of God's right hand and that of His left hand. In the third volume of the *Heidelbergsche Catechismus,* Schilder discussed Barth's suppositions and propositions. The work also contains a publication of the reports on common grace, which Schilder, together with Dr. D. H. T. Vollenhoven, had prepared for the 1939 synod of the Reformed Churches against the blind followers of Kuyper. Also in scholarly addresses after the Second World War, Schilder concerned himself with the question of whether the expression *common grace* was theologically justifiable. Despite later criticism by Dr. J. Douma,[20] I am of the opinion that Schilder correctly answered this question in the negative.

The final academic oration that Schilder delivered at the Theological Seminary in Kampen in December of 1951 is condensed in his discussion of God's providence in the fourth volume of *Heidelbergsche Catechismus*. When death approached, Schilder wrote a last note

in *De Reformatie*. In keeping with his final major topic of study, he
confessed that it is the Father's hand that opens and that closes. That
hand took Klaas Schilder from this life on March 23, 1952, to give him
rest from his labors, while his deeds will follow him (Rev. 14:13).

Schilder's Significance

Having surveyed his publications in the three periods, we may con-
clude that Schilder devoted himself to the reliable Word of the God
of the covenant in the history of mankind. That meant negatively a
fight against subjectivism and positively a fight for the acknowledg-
ment of Holy Scripture. Schilder battled against every construction
that did not do full justice to the reliability and the contents of the
Word spoken by the God of the covenant. In subjection to Holy Scripture he recognized the Reformed confessions as a good expression of
the unity of faith and a suitable means for the true unity of God's
church.

Briefly developing this conclusion further, we may think of
Schilder's definition of theology and in particular his definition of
dogmatics. Theology is the scientific knowledge of God as He reveals Himself in His Word. Dogmatics is the science that in subjection to Holy Scripture organizes and systematically treats the problems
of dogmas in a sympathetic-critical reproduction of their contents in
line with the ecumenical symbols. A comparison of these definitions
with those of Abraham Kuyper shows that Schilder wanted to do full
justice to God's Word in His revelation in Scripture. God has made
Himself known, He gave a narrative about Himself, and His account
in Holy Scripture possesses authority and clarity. God speaks to us,
and He speaks in a trustworthy manner.

Schilder defended the significance of God's revelation in history
and the reliability of the Word of the God of the covenant in a threefold manner. He did so against (1) the dialectical theology of Barth
and Brunner, (2) the scholastic elements in Kuyperian theology, and
(3) some Kuyperian ideas in the philosophy of Dooyeweerd.

In his fight against dialectical theology in particular, Schilder
returned to the theme of the reliability of God's covenant revelation

time and again. He is not haughty who bows before Holy Scripture as the trustworthy Word of the living God in the history of mankind, but he is especially haughty who, on the basis of false philosophical presuppositions, claims that the word of the Bible's authors *cannot* be the Word of God.

Already in 1927 Schilder wrote in *Bij Dichters en Schriftgeleerden* (Among Poets and Scribes),

> One should not ridicule the clarity in the revelation. Moses already referred to it (Deut. 30:11–14). He could not take his leave from this world until he had spoken of the clarity in the revelation. And the apostle Paul made this Mosaic reference to the clarity of the revealed Word into a Messianic Advent-theme, basing all of Christology on it (Rom. 10:5–9).
>
> What else could he do? For the clarity of the Word that became Scripture has been *fulfilled* in the Word become flesh. This Word incarnate has not merely twinkled, but has *dwelt* among us. It has occupied a teaching chair and has made God known to us.[21]

This was in 1927. Then in 1929 Schilder restated his position in *Tusschen "Ja" en "Neen"* (Between Yes and No) with these words:

> "To bring into the crisis," this is without a doubt seriously meant by Karl Barth. But in practice this is for many a playful euphemism for "asking for the obvious." And this is again sometimes the sin of children who know very well what father has said, but who ask it again because they secretly desire to do differently from what they were told, and is also well recognized as such: asking for the obvious, in order to be freed from it. This game in which the heart is a hypocrite before one admits it to oneself is forbidden by God, for the Word is very near you, it is in your mouth and in your heart, says Moses, when he is about to say farewell and surveys his people and its history. And so the clarity, the perspicuity, the attainability, the horizontal usefulness of the Law has been expressed clearly and comfortingly in Moses' address.[22]

In his last period, after the Second World War, Schilder addressed Dr. G. C. van Niftrik in the following manner:

> Professor van Niftrik wants to be a Barthian and Barth says of Scripture as a whole that it is a form of God's Word, one form among others. This being a "form" (*gestalte*) of God's Word is the opposite of "substance" (*gehalte*). Paradoxically, "gestalte" (form) is the opposite of "gehalte" (substance). In other words, all chapters of Scripture are honored as being a form. However, those who do not regard Scripture as one of the forms of God's Word, but as the very Word of God itself, must agree: these theologians keep all the chapters of Scripture in place, namely, as a form. But they delete them all as substance. Is saying this offensive? No, it is a sober appraisal of the situation. . . . I hope that Professor van Niftrik is no longer cross with us. We simply have no choice. And we are fighting against the obtrusive powers of unbelief, in defence of the last fortification, the reliability of God's revelation as a message of contents.[23]

Here we see the continuous theme of the trustworthiness of the words of the God of the covenant, the reliability of God's revelation in Scripture.

In his opposition to Kuyper's theory of "immediate regeneration," Schilder pointed out a failure of appreciation for the regenerating *Word*. This was also the issue in his fight against the "synodical" views of covenant and baptism. God speaks to us His promise but does not give a prediction that goes over the heads of the elect. His promise is a personal pledge; it is a message addressed to us, and it is accompanied by a command enjoining repentance and faith. Schilder remained faithful to his deep-rooted conviction in this regard also over against his friend H. Hoeksema and the Protestant Reformed Church in the United States. His brochure about the continuing danger of a suprascriptural binding (1950) was written in response to a doctrinal statement in which the Protestant Reformed Church basically identified God's covenant with God's eternal election. It has not been without significance for the history of the Canadian and American Reformed churches.[24]

Finally, also regarding his stand with respect to Dooyeweerd's *Wijsbegeerte der Wetsidee* (Philosophy of the Cosmonomic Idea),[25] it strikes us that Schilder was very sensitive to the importance of the Word that God speaks to us.

Here one may think of the criticism that he voiced concerning Dooyeweerd's concept of the faith function, the so-called pistical function. In his exposition on Lord's Day 7 of the Heidelberg Catechism, he rejected Dooyeweerd's uncritical acceptance of Abraham Kuyper's views on this matter. Here too the point is that Schilder considers God's speaking to us in history important. Our faith is a response to His revelation. Faith does not come along with God's act of creation, but it comes about through His revelation in His Word spoken to man. Schilder concludes that in Dooyeweerd's system of the philosophy of the cosmonomic idea the Word with its contents is not given the key position to which it is entitled.

One may ask whether Schilder himself was always aware of false philosophical presuppositions. Especially in his book *Wat is de Hemel?* (What Is Heaven?) he sometimes reasoned from a dualism of eternity and time that is alien to the Word of God's covenant. Nevertheless, despite his sins and weaknesses, his life and work were, by the grace of God, important for the gathering of Christ's catholic church.

Summary

Negatively speaking, we see Schilder's significance in his fight against subjectivism that replaces the normativity of Holy Scripture, and positively we see it in his acknowledgement of the reliability of God's covenantal Word in the history of mankind. He defended the revelation of the God who *speaks:* "The Word is very near you" (Deut. 30; Rom. 10).

It is a profound happiness to be Reformed, Schilder once wrote.[26] He professed this happiness in connection with his thinking about Paradise. It is a profound happiness to be Reformed also in the recognition of the Christ of the Scriptures and of the Scriptures of the Christ.

Notes

1. This article states that a national or general synod shall be held every three years.

2. The English translation of this "Declaration of Liberation or Return" can be found in *The Liberation: Causes and Consequences,* ed. Cornelis Van Dam (Winnipeg: Premier Publishing, 1995), 142–63.

3. For a biography of Schilder in English, see R. van Reest, *Schilder's Struggle for the Unity of the Church,* trans. T. Plantinga (Neerlandia, Alta., Canada: Inheritance Publications, 1990).

4. Cf. S. Greijdanus, *Sola Scriptura: Problems and Principles in Preaching Historical Texts* (Toronto: Wedge Publishing Foundation, 1970), esp. chaps. 2, 4.

5. K. Schilder, *Christ in His Suffering,* 3 vols., trans. H. Zylstra (Grand Rapids: Eerdmans, 1938).

6. K. Schilder, *Christ and Culture,* trans. G. van Rongen and W. Helder (Winnipeg: Premier, 1977). See also N. H. Gootjes, "Schilder on Christ and Culture," which forms chap. 3 of the present book.

7. J. Faber, "Kuitert en Schilder," *Lucerna* 4, no. 5 (1979): 10–20.

8. J. De Jong, *Accommodatio Dei: A Theme in K. Schilder's Theology of Revelation* (Kampen: Mondiss, 1990). See also his contribution, "Schilder on Revelation," in the present book.

9. Schilder's inaugural lecture was published in a "reconstructed form" by E. A. de Boer, *Eerste Rede, Eerste Optreden* (First Lecture, First Activity as Professor) (Franeker: van Wijnen, 1989), 39–72.

10. K. Schilder, *De Dogmatische Beteekenis der Afscheiding Ook Voor Onze Tijd* (Kampen: Kok, 1934), 41.

11. G. Puchinger, *In Memoriam Prof. Dr. K. Schilder. Gereformeerd Confessor* (Goes: Oosterbaan & Le Cointre, 1952), 21.

12. K. Schilder, *"Ons Aller Moeder"—Anno Domini 1935* (Kampen: Kok, 1935), 97.

13. K. Schilder, *"Geen Duimbreed!" Een Synodaal Besluit Inzake 't Lidmaatschap van N.S.B. en C.D.U.* (A Synodical Decision Concerning Membership of the National Socialist Movement [Beweging] and the Christian Democratic Union) (Kampen: Kok, 1936).

14. K. Schilder, "Kerkelijk Leven" (Ecclesiastical Life), *De Reformatie* 19, nos. 40–51 (1938–39); he reacted to the book of G. C. Aalders entitled *Het Verbond Gods* (The Covenant of God) (Kampen: Kok, 1939). Earlier in the same volume, Schilder had written a series of articles about the doctrine of the covenant, too. For Schilder's ideas about the covenant, see also S. A. Strauss, "Schilder on the Covenant," in the present book.

15. K. Schilder, *Heaven: What Is It?* condensed translation by M. M. Schooland (Grand Rapids: Eerdmans, 1950). On this work see the contribution of J. Kamphuis, "Schilder on Heaven," in the present book.

16. V. Hepp, *Dreigende Deformatie* (Kampen: Kok, 1937).

17. K. Schilder, "Kerkelijk Leven," *De Reformatie* 20, no. 45 (1940): 350. See also *Bezet Bezit* (Occupied Possession) (Goes: Oosterbaan & Le Cointre, 1945), 92–93. This book contains Schilder's articles against national socialism in *De Reformatie* from May to August 1940, before he was arrested and the publication of *De Reformatie* was banned.

18. The Resistance Commemoration Cross (*Verzetsherdenkingskruis*), instituted by royal decision on December 29, 1980, was posthumously given to Dr. Schilder on April 1, 1982, in recognition of "his part in the (spiritual) resistance against national socialism," according to W. G. de Vries, "Het Verzetsherdenkingskruis Posthuum Toegekend aan K. Schilder" (The Resistance Commemoration Cross Posthumously Granted to K. Schilder), *De Reformatie* 57, no. 26 (1982): 405–9.

19. K. Schilder, *Looze Kalk* (Groningen: Erven A. De Jager, 1946).

20. J. Douma, *Algemene Genade* (Common Grace) (Goes: Oosterbaan & Le Cointre, 1966).

21. K. Schilder, *Bij Dichters en Schriftgeleerden* (Amsterdam: Holland, 1927), 147.

22. K. Schilder, *Tusschen "Ja" en "Neen"* (Kampen: Kok, 1929), 358.

23. K. Schilder, *De Reformatie* 24, nos. 31–32 (1949): 255, 263. I deleted some underlinings.

24. Cf. A. C. de Jong, *The Well-meant Gospel Offer. The Views of H. Hoeksema and K. Schilder,* diss. (Franeker: Wever, 1954). T. Plantinga adds to his translation, *Schilder's Struggle for the Unity of the Church,* a chapter on North American developments and a translation (pp. 407–33) of Schilder's response to H. Hoeksema.

25. H. Dooyeweerd, *De Wijsbegeerte der Wetsidee,* 3 vols. (Amsterdam: Paris, 1935); English translation by D. H. Freeman and W. S. Young, *A New Critique of Theoretical Thought* (Philadelphia: Presbyterian and Reformed, 1953).

26. K. Schilder, *Heidelbergsche Catechismus,* 4 vols. (Goes: Oosterbaan & Le Cointre, 1947–51), 1:312: "Het is een diepe weelde, gereformeerd te zijn."

2

SCHILDER ON THE COVENANT

S. A. Strauss

Back to the Sources

Even someone who has little knowledge of Klaas Schilder would probably think that he wrote extensively about the covenant. It should
therefore be stated immediately that nowhere in any of his numerous
writings did he offer a detailed and systematic exposition of his views
on the covenant. The situation is rather that the covenant constantly
crops up in his theological writings, sometimes unexpectedly.

This state of affairs makes it very difficult to present accurately
what Schilder taught about the covenant. Since it is nearly impossible
to summarize his views regarding the covenant in a single short chapter, it will be necessary to make use of one particular secondary source.[1]
In this way Schilder's complex line of thought can be interpreted and
rendered as a logical and understandable whole. It is my hope that
this will help the reader who is not familiar with Schilder's views to
understand him more easily.

At the same time, we must not forget that the main concern of
this article is to introduce Schilder himself and his teaching on the

covenant to the reader. Therefore, the well-known maxim "back to the sources" has to be taken into account here too. Schilder, however, wrote in the Dutch language, with which most of those who speak English are not familiar. To overcome this problem, I shall translate direct quotations from the works of Schilder into English. Only when it is necessary to emphasize an important aspect will the original Dutch expression be added.

Where does one begin an investigation of the views of Schilder on the covenant? Before one takes up Schilder's writings, it is necessary first to acquire some knowledge of the course of his life. Those familiar with the Dutch language are here referred to the recently published dissertation of Dr. J. J. C. Dee.[2] The particular merit of this book is that it places Schilder's publications (up to 1934) clearly in the framework of his career. Knowing the circumstances in which each article or book was written makes it much easier to understand its contents.

For the sake of this necessary background information, a few important publications of Schilder's in which he more or less explicitly deals with the covenant are mentioned here. Already in his book about hell[3] he summarizes his view with the statement that "in the arena of preaching the covenant idea *has reserved all seats*" and that all preaching "in fact has to take its starting point in the covenant."[4] In his well-known book on heaven,[5] Schilder discusses in considerable detail the various phases of the covenant. It was at this very time that differences of opinion (about, among other things, the covenant and baptism) in the Reformed Churches in the Netherlands came to the fore, and they were put on the table of the general synod held in 1936. With enthusiasm Schilder participated in this debate. In this same year he wrote a series of meditations upon the covenant. These meditations, although already set for printing in January of 1936, were first published after his death, bearing the significant title "Alles of Niets" (All or Nothing).[6] His polemical discussions in his weekly *De Reformatie* with Prof. V. Hepp and Dr. J. Thijs also contain valuable expositions on the covenant.[7] As could be expected, Schilder wrote explicitly about the covenant several times after the Liberation in 1944. Examples include his defense against the accusations of writers from the circle of the "synodical" Reformed Churches[8] and a section in the second volume of his exposition on the Heidelberg Catechism.[9] Besides his publications, his lecture notes present valuable information on his teachings regarding the covenant. In this respect I refer to the lectures that he delivered during his first visit to the United States[10] and to the lectures in which he gives a critical discussion of the synod report that served the Reformed Churches in the Synod of 1943.[11]

Already from this short overview of the most important sources for our subject, it is apparent that Schilder was not merely an intellectual within the confines of his study. He was intensely involved in the ecclesiastical disputes of his day and developed his own viewpoints in the course of the exhausting discussions. He contended in particular with, on the one hand, the scholastic theology of Abraham Kuyper and his followers, and on the other hand, the modern theology of Karl Barth.

Schilder observed the same weakness in both schools of thought, even though this weakness arose from different motives. With regard to the doctrine of the covenant both reasoned so strongly from the perspective of the eternal decrees of God that man's responsibility in the covenant was underemphasized. In contrast, this responsibility was a basic motive in Schilder's theology: in the covenant God treats man as a responsible being and confronts him with the choice of "all or nothing," *for* God or *against* Him! Schilder therefore did everything in his power always to define the covenant in such a way that justice was done to man's responsibility. How he did this will be discussed in the following paragraphs.

Historical Reality

For his time, Schilder emphasized strongly the significance of history. The popular view of Reformed dogmaticians was that one's point of departure should be the eternal decrees of God. In opposition to this Schilder preferred (at any rate as far as the doctrine regarding the covenant is concerned) to make his point of departure the historical deeds of God. Therefore, he emphasized time and again the idea that the covenant is not just a metaphor. It is a historical reality. At the end of a summary of the debate on the covenant at that time, he states his conviction that it is essential to distinguish sharply between God's counsel of peace (*vrederaad*) and His covenant of grace and that election and covenant should not be identified. The covenant is established "in time" by means of God's Word-revelation, which results in the "real, historical" (*werkelijke, historische*) establishment of the covenant.[12]

This *point of departure* in history does not mean, of course, that Schilder denied the covenant's *background* in the suprahistorical decrees of God. On the contrary, he wrote remarkably much about the eternal decrees of God—so much that his critics often accused him of arguing from double predestination (election and reprobation) to the point that he leaned too much in the direction of supralapsarianism. It is true that certain pronouncements of Schilder's seem to substantiate such criticism. However, one who listens carefully to the whole of what Schilder wrote, specifically what he wrote about the covenant, hears him speak mostly of two aspects: God's eternal counsel (*Gods raad in de eeuwigheid*) and God's act in history (*Gods daad in de geschiedenis*). While these two truths cannot be separated, they should not be identified, either. For this reason Schilder chose to call his theological method "trinitarian-historical," that is, for the very purpose of avoiding one-sidedness.[13]

The reason why Schilder placed so much emphasis on the historical character of the covenant has to be sought once again in his own theological position. Immediately after he accepted his professorate in 1934, he delivered an important speech on the dogmatic significance of the Secession of 1834.[14] In it he crossed swords with the transcendentalistic, culture-critical, dialectical theology of K. Barth and others. He stated in this speech that those who held the Reformed view had a totally different evaluation of history.[15] If in the Canons of Dort we profess the regeneration and the perseverance of the saints, we believe that God on the one hand graciously interferes in our life vertically, but on the other hand also accompanies us horizontally. God's grace does not just touch our reality as a line touches a circle, but it enters into our existence; it brings about a *praesentia salutis* (salvation that is present). Likewise, in opposition to the followers of Kuyper, for instance with regard to their view of a justification from eternity, Schilder held to justification in time, through faith.[16]

Schilder's reflections on the significant meaning of history led him to emphasize the unity of the whole history of revelation. Even the history of Paradise, before the fall into sin, constituted no *pre*historical time! Therefore, it was on the basis of "the presupposition of faith" that Schilder traced the history of the covenant back to the so-called covenant of works. In the doctrine of the covenant, as in all other chapters of dogmatics, we have to start at the beginning. It is there that we learn the fundamental structure of the covenant. That which was to follow— for instance, the covenant with Abraham, or that with Israel at Sinai, or the new covenant in Christ—is not *another* covenant but only other *phases* of one and the same covenant. Characteristically, Schilder phrases his insight in this way:

> The covenant of grace is not a second covenant, for God does not duplicate. As a matter of fact, duplications are at variance with the covenant; a covenant stands or falls with the precept "all or nothing," and therefore also with "always or never" (*immer of nimmer*), as well as with "once and for all" (*eens en voor altijd*).[17]

Category of Continuity

Schilder's emphasis on the covenant as a historical reality enabled him to see correctly that which can be described as the category of *continuity* between the various phases of the covenant. With this term I mean that Schilder did not see the relation between the various phases of the covenant as one of identity. For this would deny the progressive line of the history of the covenant (from the *proton,* the very beginning in Paradise, to the *eschaton,* the very end in the new heaven and earth). But he also always refused to acknowledge any contradiction between the various dispensations of the covenant, for this would again ignore the fundamental unity of the history of the covenant.[18]

Due to these basic convictions, Schilder wrote extensively about the so-called covenant of works. The biblical foundation for this he saw especially in the parallel drawn by Paul between Adam and Christ,

the Second Adam (Rom. 5:12; 1 Cor. 15:45). It was his conviction
that we can understand but little of the covenant of grace unless we
start at the beginning, the covenant of works. The covenant of grace,
in fact, constitutes a continuation of the covenant of works. Therefore, he points out various similarities between the covenant of works
and the covenant of grace. There are, in fact, no differences in essence between the two; there is only a difference in method or means.
This difference concerns the way in which the covenant is realized.
Since the fall into sin, this is accomplished through the promised
Mediator (Gen. 3:15) and in the way of faith in Him.[19]

Schilder applies the category of continuity in a similar way when
he discusses the relation between the old covenant (before Christ)
and the new covenant (after Christ). This subject was discussed extensively at the time. Following Calvin, traditional Reformed theology has always underlined the unity of substance and, at the same time,
the difference in administration between the two dispensations of the
covenant. However, the Reformed theology of later years, as prac-
ticed by the followers of Kuyper, was all too much inclined to assume
a contrast between the old covenant and the new, as if the former was
a covenant characterized by the law and the latter was a covenant
characterized by the gospel.

Schilder objected vehemently to this viewpoint. In his comprehensive response to Dr. J. Thijs he enters into this matter.[20] Appealing to the earlier Reformed theologians, he states his conviction that
the difference between the old covenant and the new cannot be expressed in terms of external and internal. It is rather a matter of less
and more richness with regard to what has been revealed about both
the external and the internal blessings.[21] For this reason we have to
watch that we do not claim, as Thijs does, that the old covenant was
bilateral, and therefore could be broken, while this is not the case
with the new covenant. No, in the new covenant also God punishes,
and this even more severely, the disobedience of His covenant people
with the wrath of the covenant. Therefore, the threat of the covenant
is still an essential element in the dispensation of the new covenant.
For this reason it is Schilder's view that true "covenant preaching
presents the strongest appeal to human responsibility. This is why
such preaching is also so tremendously serious, and revealing . . .

comforting, but destroying all excuses for idleness [*maar met stuk-snijding van alle duivels-oorkussens*]."[22] Such covenant preaching is a prohibition against imagining going to hell while being on the way to heaven, and it is a prevention against imagining going to heaven while being on the way to hell.[23]

In this way Schilder dealt with the category of continuity in his treatment of the history of the covenant. That such an approach holds certain consequences for the preaching and for the spiritual life in the church is immediately evident. Whoever is able to preach in such a manner within a covenant framework will surely rouse the congregation from a false sense of security. This aspect is a fundamental characteristic of Schilder's views on the covenant.

Two Parties

Especially after the Synod of 1936, the structure of the covenant was a constant subject for discussion and dispute in Reformed circles. Schilder summarized the questions that were discussed and about which there was such a difference of opinion as follows.[24] (1) Who are in the covenant of grace: the elect only, or also others? (2) Does the covenant contain conditions, or not? (3) Is the covenant unilateral (*monopleurisch*) or bilateral (*dipleurisch*)? (4) Can the covenant of grace ever be broken from the side of God? (5) Can the new covenant be broken from the side of man? (6) Is there covenant wrath in the new covenant? (7) Should one distinguish between essence and appearance in the covenant? (8) With whom is the covenant established: with Christ or with God's people?

Initially Schilder concurred with the generally accepted Reformed view that the covenant is unilateral (*monopleurisch*) in its origin and bilateral (*dipleurisch*) in its existence. Gradually, however, he placed more and more emphasis on the bilateral character of the covenant, just because his opponents underestimated this aspect. He found special support for the fact that the covenant indeed has two parties (God and man) in the biblical pronouncement that we are "God's fellow workers" ("co-workers" [1 Cor. 3:9]). In his debate with Dr. O. Noordmans, in 1936, he dealt extensively with this matter. In his exposition he states that the preposition "co[n]" (meaning "together with") in the term "co-workers" should not be interpreted figuratively. Particularly in the covenant, this preposition receives a very literal meaning: unilaterally God creates a bilateral relation between Himself and us.[25]

One year later, Prof. V. Hepp openly launched an attack against all those who called the covenant bilateral. In his response to Hepp,[26] Schilder emphatically stated that Reformed theology has always taught that the covenant has two parties (God and man). Whoever wants to deny this truth cuts into the very nerves of the concept of the covenant. Without ever denying the unilateral origin of the covenant, one has to maintain its bilateral existence with unfaltering conviction. In short, the covenant *is* bilateral; it is a mutual agreement between *two* parties, albeit two immeasurably *unequal* parties.[27]

Why did Schilder defend this point of view so vehemently? He did so to make it fully clear that, in the covenant, God treats man as an actual and responsible partner. Man is not a nonentity in the covenant; he most definitely counts.[28] Giving man a position of accountability, says Schilder, forms part of the constitution of the covenant.[29] The appeal to our responsibility constitutes one of the essential elements of the covenant.[30] How important Schilder regarded this matter can be underlined by the following flowery pronouncement: "People sometimes make bears dance on a heated floor. One can also regard the covenant in this way. It fans the flames to great heat. Nothing makes us more responsible. In the covenant our responsibility is infinitely strengthened."[31]

It is evident, then, that Schilder found no difficulty in simultaneously maintaining both the unilateral origin and the bilateral existence of the covenant. Without detracting from God's sovereign dispensation of the covenant, Schilder insisted that we may never speak of predestination in such a way that it undermines our human responsibility. He once said in a sermon that the biblical pronouncement "your Maker is your husband" (Isa. 54:5) "constitutes the ABC of the doctrine of the covenant." By His sheer grace God makes us—lost sinners—His people. But then He proceeds to enter into a bilateral relationship with us, like a husband with his wife.[32]

Since the covenant constitutes a bilateral relationship, it implies a "mutual obligation" on the part of both parties. Early Reformed theologians took this term from their colleagues in the Faculty of Law.[33] Schilder regarded it as an argument in favor of his position that the covenant, as a bilateral relationship, has a legal character. He saw this as a very important matter. Unceasingly he emphasized the point that the covenant is a *legal* arrangement that confers a *legal* status upon the members of the covenant people. Of course, this does not mean that the covenant is a mere legal contract between God and man. This would be a heretical thought. God's covenant with us constitutes a covenant of grace! But, so Schilder says, in the covenant God's gifts of love come to us in a legal relationship and with legal guarantees (*rechtsgaranties*). Love and legal rights go hand in hand; this is why I have the right to pull at the hem of God's robe.[34]

This legal character of the covenant has, in the view of Schilder, at least two important consequences. On the one hand, it implies that the promises of God come to us in the covenant with the sure guarantee that a legal relation can offer us. On the other hand, it means that the demands with which God, who forms the other party in the covenant, comes to us must be regarded just as seriously. He has the fullest right to enter into a "lawsuit" against His people, as the Old Testament prophets repeatedly proclaimed. Herewith we have already touched upon the subject of the next paragraphs.

Two Parts

We have learned by now how Schilder responded to some of the questions regarding the covenant as he summarized them. The covenant is a bilateral relationship with a legal character. Deserving our attention next are the elements that together constitute the covenant. In agreement with the Reformed Form for Baptism, Schilder refers on this point to the two parts of the covenant, namely, promise and demand. However, it was characteristic for Schilder that he added to these two the sanctions (*sancties*) of the covenant, namely, the assurance of reward in the way of faith and the threat of punishment in the case of unbelief and disobedience.[35] Schilder regarded these elements of promise (with the assurance of reward) and demand (with the threat of wrath) as parts of the substance of the covenant that were present in all the different phases of the history of the covenant. The wrath of the covenant (Lev. 26:25) is, therefore, not just something that occurred only in the old covenant dispensation. It undoubtedly also characterizes, according to Schilder, the new covenant in Christ. Thus, these elements also serve to underline his basic conviction regarding the covenant, namely, that it emphasizes the responsibility of man.

The question can now be asked whether such an emphasis upon the responsibility of man does not undermine the certainty of the covenant. Schilder replied in the negative. Precisely because the covenant comes to us with legal warranties (*rechtsassuranties*), it stimulates our trust of faith in Him who gives us His promises. However, the promise of the covenant may never be separated from its demand. Promise and demand are absolutely correlated in the covenant. If one would separate the promise from the demand, he would change the promise into a mere prediction. If, on the other hand, one would separate the demand from the promise, he would introduce a new law with a legalistic character. Schilder writes that it is entirely impossible to separate these two parts, promise and demand, from each other, just as in the marriage bond husband and wife may not be put asunder.[36]

How the two parts of the covenant function in the lives of the people of the covenant can be explained with what Schilder wrote about baptism. For baptism seals, in a sacramental way, the *promise* of the gospel.[37] But this promise, in fact, *demands* from us that we, in faith, appropriate for ourselves what is promised, and so make it our own. Due to this state of affairs, Schilder did not hesitate to speak about faith as a condition in the covenant. Of course, this does not mean *condition* in the Arminian sense of the word, as if man could earn something through his obedience, but *condition* in the Reformed sense. Faith, he writes,[38] is indeed a gift of the God of the covenant, but it is, at the same time, also a condition set by Him. Evidently the concept *condition* can be interpreted in more than one sense. What Schilder had in mind with his "Reformed doctrine of conditions"[39] is that God has decreed that salvation can never be realized without faith. One's baptism, therefore, does not imply a dogmatic proclamation, for instance, that God confers salvation on the elect. But in my baptism I receive a concrete address from God, a message that God proclaims to everyone who is baptized, personally: if you believe, you will be saved.

Lasting Significance

It is a fact that Schilder's theology was very much a product of his time. The pronouncements that are characteristic for him, also with regard to the covenant, were determined by the theological debates of his time to such an extent that one has to be careful not to quote him out of context. Nevertheless, it cannot be denied that on certain points he made a contribution so valuable that it can help us still today to understand better what the Word of God reveals to us with regard to the covenant.

The emphasis that Schilder laid on the covenant as a historical reality is a matter for which modern theologians can express only appreciation. Someone like Dr. H. Berkhof expressly associates himself with it.[40] But Schilder did not emphasize only the bilateral existence of the covenant in history. As we saw, he also maintained its unilateral origin in eternity. For this aspect modern theology does not have much appreciation. These days there exists a tendency to reject any reference to the eternal decrees as "metaphysical" and to refuse to connect them with the covenant in any way. However, we cannot accept such a point of view, for it renders our salvation too uncertain and opens the door wide for all kinds of Arminian ideas. If the covenant is no longer founded on God's eternal decrees, the question of whether man will be included in the covenant or not ultimately depends on man's own free choice It is obvious that in such circles the doctrine of infant baptism, which is so closely associated with the doctrine of the covenant, will also be exchanged for an Anabaptistic view.

One does not have to agree in every respect with Schilder's exposition of double predestination in which the covenant, too, is founded. Criticism of it has appeared.[41] However, what we should continue to thank Schilder for is his showing us a way in which we can profess both the eternal decrees of God and the covenant as a historical reality. He taught us not to identify election and covenant. Therefore, we have to distinguish between the covenant of salvation (which was established with Christ and, in Him, with all the elect, from eternity) and the covenant of grace (which was established with the believers and their children in time). By doing so, we can, together with the Canons of Dort (chap. 1), confess election and, at the same time, say that the *promise* of the gospel must be proclaimed without exception to all mankind together with the *demand* of conversion and faith (chap. 2, par. 5). As Schilder has shown, the confession of God's eternal election and reprobation never takes away the responsibility of man.

Likewise, Schilder's point of view regarding the two-sidedness of the covenant is still relevant today. In Berkhof's opinion,[42] the modern concept of "intersubjectivity" is well suited to give a description of the relationship between the two parties of the covenant. For this reason he has an open mind to the concept of human responsibility and cooperation in the covenant. We should ask, however, whether this modern emphasis on the partnership between God and man is the same as that expounded by Schilder in his time. This question must be answered with great caution. The tendency exists in modern theology to exchange the sovereignty and self-sufficiency of God for an image of God based on a concept of "covenantal" partnership that implies that He cannot fully realize Himself as God without man's involvement. This is most definitely not what Schilder taught. His view of the covenant can teach us also in this respect that one can indeed fully acknowledge the responsibility of man without detracting in the least from the sovereignty of God.

What Schilder wrote about the correlation between the promise and the demand of the covenant was not always thankfully received. It sounds so contrary to the gospel to attach as much emphasis to the demand of the covenant as to the promise of the covenant. Such a point of view can easily cause people to think that the promise is of no value unless one first has met the demand. He who reasons in this way does in fact subscribe to a subjectivistic view of the covenant, as if the covenant is established only when the sinner has come to conversion and faith. I really do not believe that Schilder incorporated some hidden form of Methodism into his doctrine of the covenant.

What he in fact wanted to emphasize with all his strength is that the covenant should never be allowed to lead to a false sense of security. People of the covenant may never think that salvation is already theirs because they have received the promise. The promises of the covenant are not predictions; they imply demands. But these demands must be seen as demands of the covenant, not as simple prerequisites that one can meet in one's own strength. After all, the link between promise and demand is to be found in the one Word of God, which has come from God: comforting, but also threatening.

This is, then, the great and lasting significance of what Schilder taught us about the covenant. When God establishes His covenant with human persons, He treats them as responsible beings. As Schilder characteristically put it, the covenant stands or falls by its rule "all or nothing."

Notes

1. S. A. Strauss, *Alles of Niks: K. Schilder Oor die Verbond* (All or Nothing: K. Schilder on the Covenant), diss. (Bloemfontein, South Africa: Patmos, 1986).

2. J. J. C. Dee, *K. Schilder: Zijn Leven en Werk. Deel I. 1890–1934* (K. Schilder: His Life and Work, vol. 1), diss. (Goes: Oosterbaan & Le Cointre, 1990).

3. K. Schilder, *Wat is de Hel?* (What Is Hell?) (Kampen: Kok, 1932), 185–97.

4. Ibid., 188.

5. K. Schilder, *Wat is de Hemel?* (What Is Heaven?) (Kampen: Kok, 1935), 237–68.

6. K. Schilder, *Verzamelde Werken, Deel II. Schriftoverdenkingen* (Collected Writings, part II. Meditations) (Goes: Oosterbaan & Le Cointre, 1957), 91–185.

7. See K. Schilder, "Prof. Hepps Misverstanden Inzake de Algemeene Genade" (Prof. Hepp's Misunderstandings in the Matter of Common Grace), *De Reformatie* 18, nos. 6–23 (1937–38). The reaction to J. Thijs began with K. Schilder, "Verborgene en Geopenbaarde Dingen" (Concealed and Revealed Things [about election and the covenant]), *De Reformatie* 18, nos. 38–44, 50–53 (1938); 19, nos. 1–7 (1938).

8. K. Schilder, *Looze Kalk* (Untempered Mortar) (Groningen, the Netherlands: De Jager, 1946).

9. K. Schilder, *Heidelbergsche Catechismus,* 4 vols. (Goes: Oosterbaan & Le Cointre, 1947–51), 2:499–520.

10. K. Schilder, *Americana. Verslag van de in Amerika Gehouden Lezingen, op Verzoek van de Studenten Herhaald op de Colleges van april–juni 1939* (Americana. A Report of the Speeches Held in the United States, Repeated at the Request of the Students in Lectures from April to June 1939) (Kampen: Library of the Theological University). These are lecture notes made and published by Schilder's students without the authority of Schilder.

11. K. Schilder, *Dogmahistorie Praeadvies—Intermezzo College Dogmatiek over het Praeadvies van Commissie I, 1943* (History of Dogma: Preadvice. Intermezzo Lecture in Dogmatics About the Pre-Advice of Committee I, 1943); these are unofficially published lecture notes.

12. K. Schilder, "Is er Eenstemmigheid over het Genadeverbond?" (Is There Consensus on the Covenant of Grace?), *De Reformatie* 21, nos. 6–9; the references and citations are from vol. 21, no. 9, p. 65.

13. Schilder, *Heidelbergsche Catechismus,* 3:7.

14. K. Schilder, *De Dogmatische Beteekenis der Afscheiding Ook Voor Onze Tijd* (The Dogmatic Significance of the Secession Also for Our Time) (Kampen: Kok, 1934); also published in K. Schilder, *Verzamelde Werken, Deel III, De Kerk,* (Collected Writings, part III. The Church) (Goes: Oosterbaan & Le Cointre, 1962), 2:7–76.

15. Schilder, *Verzamelde Werken: De Kerk,* 34, 38 [= *De Dogmatische Beteekenis,* 35, 39].

16. Strauss, *Alles of Niks,* 70.

17. Schilder, *Wat is de Hemel?,* 252.

18. Strauss, *Alles of Niks,* 112.

19. Ibid., 96; see also K. Schilder, *Het Verbond in de Gereformeerde Symbolen* (The Covenant in the Reformed Standards) (lecture notes published independently by Schilder's students), 9.

20. See the series of articles in *De Reformatie* 18, nos. 38–44, 50–53 (1938); 19, nos. 1–7 (1938).

21. *De Reformatie* 18, no. 43 (1938): 383–84.

22. *De Reformatie* 19, no. 7 (1938): 51.

23. Strauss, *Alles of Niks,* 111, referring to two sermons of Schilder, in C. Veenhof, ed., *Om Woord en Kerk* (For the Sake of Word and Church) (Goes: Oosterbaan & Le Cointre, 1948), vol. 1. The first appears on pp. 80–104, and the second, "De Lastering Tegen de Heilige Geest" (The Sin of Blasphemy Against the Holy Spirit), appears on pp. 205–30. See also Schilder, *Heidelbergsche Catechismus,* 1:461–72.

24. *De Reformatie* 21, nos. 7–8 (1945), 49–50, 57–58.

25. Strauss, *Alles of Niks,* 130; see the discussion in *De Reformatie* 16, no. 10 (1935), introduction, nos. 15 and 16 (1936; O. Noordmans's article on common grace), and nos. 17, 18, 20–27, 30–34, 36–37 (1936; the response of Schilder); this discussion is reprinted in G. Puchinger, *Een Theologie in Discussie* (A Theology in Discussion) (Kampen: Kok, 1970).

26. *De Reformatie* 18, esp. no. 40 (1938): 358.

27. Strauss, *Alles of Niks,* 138, and Schilder, *Heidelbergsche Catechismus,* 1:317–20.

28. Schilder, *Heidelbergsche Catechismus,* 1:321.

29. Ibid., 3:365.

30. Schilder, *Looze Kalk,* 52.

31. Schilder, *Americana,* 11.

32. Strauss, *Alles of Niks,* 141; see also K. Schilder, *Verzamelde Werken. Preken* (Goes: Oosterbaan & Le Cointre, 1955), 3:44.

33. Strauss, *Alles of Niks,* 147, referring to *De Reformatie* 18, no. 8 (1937): 98.

34. Schilder, *Americana,* 16.

35. Strauss, *Alles of Niks,* 157, with reference to *De Reformatie* 18, no. 8 (1937): 98–99, and Schilder, *Looze Kalk,* 12, 37.

36. Schilder, *Looze Kalk,* 60–61.

37. Cf. Heidelberg Catechism, Question and Answer 66.

38. Schilder, *Looze Kalk,* 61.

39. Strauss, *Alles of Niks,* 183; also Schilder, *Heidelbergsche Catechismus,* 2:344, 349.

40. H. Berkhof, *Christelijk Geloof. Een Inleiding to de Geloofsleer* (Nijkerk: Callenbach, 1973), translated by S. Woudstra as *The Christian Faith. An Introduction to the Study of the Faith* (Grand Rapids: Eerdmans, 1979), 178.

41. Strauss, *Alles of Niks,* 188–96.

42. Berkhof, *The Christian Faith,* 217.

3

Schilder on Christ and Culture

N. H. Gootjes

Introduction

To pay attention to culture in a commemoration of K. Schilder needs no defense. Schilder was very interested in culture, but this can be said about many people. Far more important is the fact that he defined culture in such a way that it should interest every Christian. Everyone who believes in God and in Jesus Christ cannot but say, "There is not an inch of the whole area of our human life about which Christ, who is Sovereign of all, does not proclaim, 'Mine.'"

This sentence of Kuyper's reflects Schilder's own conviction. Schilder emphasized his belief that the people of God should be culturally active.[1] And many Reformed believers have listened to him. Much activity in the Reformed Churches from the fifties onward can be explained against the background of Schilder's rousing words on culture. Even the expression *cultural mandate,* the summary expression for this activity, was in all probability coined by Schilder. Schilder's views on culture were very influential.

At the same time, Schilder's view of culture has been, and still is, one of the most controversial aspects of his theology. Dr. O. Noord-mans criticized the article in which Schilder had explained his opin-ion in a speech given for the theological students at the Free University of Amsterdam. Schilder then invited him to publish his views in *De Reformatie,* the weekly edited by Schilder. Noordmans wrote about his first impressions upon reading Schilder's article on culture,

> I wondered whether this is still the same faith in which I was educated, or whether a new religion is growing here, which claims to have its origin in the Reformed roots, but which is so much different from anything we saw there up to now, that the question cannot be suppressed whether it does not draw its sap from a different gospel.

Noordmans's first impression, that Schilder's view of culture had no foundation in the gospel, was confirmed by the time he reached the end of his articles. There he called it "this absolutizing of the doctrine of common grace, this desecration of Scripture."[2]

Noordmans, however, did not belong to the Reformed Churches, to which Schilder belonged. But also within the Reformed Churches Schilder was faced with opposition. A major opponent was Schilder's colleague at the Free University, Dr. V. Hepp. His opinion was that Schilder's view of culture belonged to the deformation which was threatening the church in his day.[3]

Criticism of Schilder's views on culture has continued, even though it is not as fierce today as it was in the beginning. But these are still some of the most widely debated and rejected of Schilder's convictions. To give just one example, in April of 1990 the Free Uni-versity organized a symposium on various aspects of Schilder's work. The impression of one of the attendants was that *Christ and Culture* was virtually the only publication of Schilder's about which no one had said a positive word. And in many articles and lectures published during the commemoration year, Schilder's view of culture has been criticized.[4]

It therefore seems good once more to confront ourselves with this important part of Schilder's heritage. We will concentrate on the central issue, the cultural mandate itself.[5] What was this view that on the one hand was enthusiastically followed and on the other hand was strongly rejected? Schilder cannot be understood without Dr. A. Kuyper, who almost single-handedly developed a world-and-life-view for the Reformed Churches and organized life accordingly. After briefly considering Kuyper's thoughts on culture, we will return to Schilder.

Kuyper on "Culture"

The Reformed world as it existed around 1920, with its outreach in many directions, was the creation of Kuyper. And yet his books give the impression that culture was not important for him. He hardly mentions it in his many works. Culture is not even mentioned where it could be expected. A case in point is his famous lectures on Calvinism. Kuyper dealt with the topics "Calvinism and politics," "Calvinism and academic studies," and "Calvinism and art," but there was no lecture on Calvinism and culture.[6]

The reason is that Kuyper was not happy with the word *culture*. The word is connected with the idea of cultivation. Therefore, it is used, according to Kuyper, by people who do not begin with God, but with man. Man is like a farmer who does all the planting, who takes care of the plants, and who removes everything that would stunt the growth. In culture man is seen as the one who develops his life to a higher level. Since the word *culture* is man-centered, Kuyper wants to use the term *common grace* instead. According to him, Calvin and our Reformed fathers spoke of common grace, because they began with God. God softens our misery, and He makes possible the development of human powers in all fields.[7]

This sheds a very particular light on culture. According to Kuyper, culture is a matter of grace, the result of an undeserved gift from God in a world full of sin. Even in this sinful world we see much development and great cultural achievements. How is this possible? Cultural development is first of all the result of common grace. And because this grace is common, culture is not the specialty of God's people; it has developed everywhere. At the same time it must be admitted that a culture based on common grace is very limited. Only the addition of special grace will enable culture to reach its full growth.

The best way to understand this view of Kuyper's is to follow the historical exposition that he gives.[8] He begins by drawing attention to the fact that great civilizations have existed in China and Japan, in America and India. Highly developed human societies have been established in these countries. Kuyper sees here a cultural development that was completely independent of the Christian religion. These cultures were the result of common grace alone. But this cultural development remained unfulfilled. Its strength was broken halfway through its progress.

The history of these nations shows this clearly. Highly developed civilizations existed in Mexico and Peru. But these civilizations have now completely disappeared, and the cultures of the Indians in these countries no longer exist. In India the situation is different. Its highly developed culture is partly still existent. There is still a possibility for it to grow into new bloom. But its growth is stunted—it is no longer developing. This country, instead of developing its own culture, imports the results of Western culture (railroads, the telegraph, and so on).

An even clearer example of stunted growth can be found in China and Japan. In these countries we find orderly societies, high levels of artistic and intellectual development, and prosperity. In Kuyper's words, "The fruit of common grace among these nations was very abundant." But the development was limited. In the first place, the result of common grace was limited to these nations themselves. The human race as a whole did not benefit from their cultures. And in the second place, these civilizations do not show lasting profit. When they meet Western civilization, the national cultures seem to wither.

Common grace, therefore, has only a limited influence upon the nations; it is limited in place and in time. It blesses some populations, while other nations do not benefit from it. And even in the populations that it does reach, culture develops only to a certain extent. Then the culture either declines or petrifies.

But there is also a development of common grace that has not been limited to one particular nation but is destined to bless every nation. This development is also not limited to a certain period; it continues throughout all ages. This development did not get stuck at a certain level, but it can always develop further. This is the development of common grace that began in Babylon and Egypt, flourished to a certain extent in Greece and Rome, and was then assimilated by Christianity. And under the cross of Christ it has continued to develop throughout all centuries.

Kuyper means here that common grace, as it was present in Greece and Rome, was a preparation for the Christian religion. When Christianity was added to the culture of Greece and Rome, this culture blossomed into unprecedented development. The expansion of Western culture is the result of Christ's government. Christ's work did not end with His ascension from the Mount of Olives. It has a new beginning in His sitting at the right hand of the Father. Christ has added Christian religion to the Greek-Roman culture. Common grace, as it has worked in the roots of Western civilization, has reached far greater heights because of the particular grace of Christ.[9]

The special character of Western culture can now be explained. Here the saving work of Christ (particular grace) and the development of civilization are not separate, but have become one. Christ's saving work does not bring about a new world separate from Western civilization; it develops this civilization. "It is and remains the same ancient world once created by God, which is preserved by common grace, and which is restored in its life core and purged of the cancer in its root, by particular grace."[10]

All other civilizations have either disappeared or had their power broken. But since the church of the New Testament has been entrusted with leading the nations, common grace always opens new avenues under the influence of the Christian religion. The Christian world of Europe and America is the highest development of our human race in all history, and it seems to be destined to develop even further.[11]

Looking back at this view of Kuyper's, we cannot but be impressed by the stunning perspective that he has opened on world history.[12] The saving work of Jesus Christ is in this view not limited to saving souls or saving persons. Christ came to save culture too. He took the culture of Greece and Rome and infused into it the powers of Christianity. As a result, the classical culture was healed of the deadly disease that sapped the strength of all other cultures. This is the reason why Western culture could rise higher than any other civilization. Kuyper was now able to explain the difference between the backwardness of other civilizations and the progress of Western civilization. The theologian Kuyper here became the cultural historian Kuyper.

The result is, of course, that there is no Christian culture. There is only a Western culture influenced by Christianity. We do not have to work towards a Christian culture; we have to work towards further Christianization of Western culture. Kuyper's activities in politics and for higher education cannot be separated from this view of culture. The Anti-Revolutionary Party and the Free University were the means to develop Western society in a more Christian direction.[13]

Between Kuyper and Schilder

About thirty-five years separate Schilder's article on cultural life from Kuyper's *Common Grace*. Much changed during that time. The almost boundless trust people of Kuyper's days had in the greatness of Western culture was shattered. Germany, the greatest cultural power on the European continent, had begun a disastrous war. The First World War had shown that progress in science and art does not automatically mean progress in civilization. When even the leading nation in philosophy (Germany) could commit such barbarous atrocities, it was difficult to look optimistically at Western culture and to maintain that this culture is the direct result of Christian influence on ancient civilization. After the war Western civilization was in a crisis.[14]

In the Reformed Churches in the Netherlands, however, it looked as if life went on as before. The political party and the university that Kuyper had founded were flourishing. The party could again boast a strong leader in H. Colijn, who served as prime minister several times. The Free University was expanding; departments were added, and the number of students increased. Yet there was also uneasiness about cultural questions. In this situation it was the theologian K. Schilder who pointed to a new direction.

The Importance of Christ

Not only Kuyper, but also Schilder begins with Jesus Christ in connection with culture. His original article was entitled "Jesus Christ and Cultural Life." When the expanded version was published as a book, the title was shortened but the reference to Jesus Christ was maintained: *Christ and Culture*. Both works begin with an extensive discussion of the importance of Jesus Christ for culture.

Schilder follows here the explanation of the Heidelberg Catechism. *Jesus* is the name that indicates that He had come to be the Savior. The essence of His office is to save. But He is not just Jesus, He is also the Christ. This part of His name means that He has been officially appointed by God to be the Savior.[15] Jesus Christ should be seen as the Savior also in connection with culture. He is making a number of rebellious people into people of God. They are not perfect, and yet they are purified and therefore taken into the service of God. In this sense it is Christ's duty "to conquer the world for God." The earth should be brought back to its rightful owner. For that purpose Christ renews those who are anointed together with Him, the Christians.[16]

Even though both Kuyper and Schilder begin with Jesus Christ when they speak of culture, they have different views on His significance for culture. Kuyper sees Jesus Christ as a Savior who pours out His special grace into Greek-Roman culture, that is to say, Jesus Christ is the Savior of culture. But Schilder sees Jesus Christ as the Savior of man. He works salvation in many. This work includes making disobedient people into people who serve God again in their cultural work.[17]

Back to the Beginning

Christ the Savior brings His people back to their duty. What then is this duty? Where can it be found? According to Schilder, the duty is that of Paradise.[18] The duty is given in the words that God spoke to man after he was created, in Genesis 1:28: "Fill the earth and subdue it." This duty is also expressed in the words spoken about man after he was placed in the Garden of Eden, in Genesis 2:15, "to till it and keep it." God did not create a world that was fully developed. Man in Paradise had to work as God's fellow worker.

God gave this command in the beginning, but man sinned. In his sin man no longer wants to obey God and His Word. In his disobedience man cannot escape the structures that God has created in this world; he has to follow God's natural laws. But man can be disobedient to God's moral law,[19] and in fact, he does not obey God. He works in this world in disobedience to his Creator. Then Christ interferes. As Savior He works regeneration. The conviction of Schilder is that Christ does His merciful work also for cultural life.[20] Christ also confronts man again with God's command set in place from the beginning. Man, therefore, has to do cultural work.[21]

Culture

This brings us to the question of what culture is in Schilder's view. But here everyone feels helpless. Schilder summarized his view of culture in one complex sentence that takes up half a page.[22] We will content ourselves with highlighting some very important aspects.

First, culture is the totality of the work to be done in this world.[23] The word *culture* is derived from a Latin verb that means "to cultivate." All the work a farmer does on his land to get a good harvest can be called culture.[24] Schilder connects this with the mandate from the beginning to till the Garden and keep it (Gen. 2:15). He then extends its meaning in such a way that culture includes everything that is done to keep and develop the earth.

Culture should not be limited to the world of art, according to Schilder, or to art and scholarship. Of course, these too belong to culture. Schilder is not afraid to tell the Reformed people that developing the arts belongs to our duty before God. But art is not the only cultural work in this world. A professor, too, should do his work as cultural work. The garbage collector also does cultural work, as does the housewife. Actually, every type of work to be done on this earth belongs to culture.[25]

A second important aspect of Schilder's view of culture is his belief that the cultural mandate implies that the world has to be developed. The world was created good, but it was not created in a fully developed form. God has made a world with many possibilities. Man has to work so that the possibilities can become realities. In this sense Schilder speaks of evolution on the basis of creation.[26]

To give an example, God prepared a garden for man, but this one garden would not be enough when children and grandchildren would be born. More land had to be cultivated. Therefore, a spade was needed. To develop a spade, head and hand had to cooperate; the head to invent it, the hand to use it.[27] Technical inventions belong to the culture that man had to develop. The world will change as a result of man's cultural work. Culture will mean a development from garden to city.[28]

A third important characteristic of culture is that it is the duty of all mankind. The cultural mandate was first given to Adam and Eve in Paradise. It then came to their offspring. All humans should be involved in cultural work. Or perhaps it is better to say that all men should do their daily work as cultural work. They are all creatures made by God. While living on this earth, they should labor in God's service on God's earth. But many do not work in this way. This is one reason why cultural development, the development of this world, will never be completed. Those who reject God use the materials that God has created and work with the abilities that God has given them, but without obeying God. As a result of this disobedience much of their cultural work will be spoiled. In the end it will become evident that their cultural achievements are only torsos, truncated pyramids.[29]

Of course, there are also the regenerated. With them a beginning of obedience in cultural work should become visible. But this, too, will not lead to a completed cultural development. Christian culture, too, is left with truncated pyramids.[30] Several reasons can be given for this. First is the fact that they are a minority. Only a few people are left to do a work that was to be performed by all. They simply do not have enough manpower to do what should be done in this world.[31] Another reason is the sin that is still present in them. It can be a duty for a Christian not to engage in a certain type of work, because his eye or hand can lead him into sin.[32]

The last aspect that has to be mentioned here is that culture always should be to the glory of God. When man sinned, he broke away from God. His cultural activity became, from that moment onward, separated from God. Cultural development became an end in itself. Separated from God, products of culture can even become dangerous. A hammer is a useful instrument, but hammers have been used to harm and to kill.[33]

Sin also gives a wrong perspective on culture. In this view, for example, sports become something of first importance instead of a pastime. Schilder says that even in so-called Christian newspapers, four columns are devoted to sports but only half a column is devoted to church news. The winner of a match is mentioned in large print, but not a word is devoted to the spiritual struggle.[34] But the glory of God should determine the importance of everything.

Enough has been said to show that Schilder's view of culture is far from abstract. It is not as broad in scope as that of Kuyper. It does not attempt to survey the whole history of the world in one sweeping overview. But it reaches deeper than Kuyper's view. It penetrates the heart and encourages every Christian to perform his daily work as a mandate from God.

Schilder's view has received severe criticism.[35] In the following paragraphs we will have a look at some recent criticisms and try to evaluate them.

Foundation in Scripture

More than once it has been said that the cultural mandate as Schilder spoke about it has no foundation in Scripture. Recently someone called it a "soap bubble." The cultural mandate looks nice, but when you touch it, it has no scriptural content. It breaks and disappears. This is, of course, the most severe criticism that can be levelled against a Reformed theologian. We have therefore to pay some attention to the texts that underlie Schilder's understanding.[36]

Schilder's main proof was what God said in connection with the creation of man in Genesis 1 and 2. For the salvation of Jesus Christ means that the Christian is brought back to the original obedience required of him after his creation. What did God say at the beginning of our history?

In Genesis 1:26 God speaks to Himself about creating man. God wants to make man in such a way that he will have dominion over the fish of the sea, the birds of the air, and all the animals on the land. The word meaning "to have dominion" is very remarkable here. We usually find it in the Bible with the connotation of violently subduing someone. But that cannot be the meaning in Genesis 1, because God said this in the beginning of the world, in the period before sin. The verb can also mean "to use as a slave" (Isa. 14:2). If we remove the negative connotation, I think this meaning fits Genesis 1. The animals that God has created have to become servants of man.

Let us give a few examples. The cow has been created; it exists in the created world. But it wanders around freely. Man is given the right to domesticate it and to use its milk. The horse too has been created; it is galloping about in Eden. Man has the right and the ability to catch it, to tame it, to bridle it, and to ride it. Imagine what a development this means to created man. He can go more quickly than he could on his own feet, and he can carry heavier loads. But also imagine how much man has to invent to do this, even in a sinless world. He has to invent the bridle, reins, the wheel and a cart, stables, and fences. All this belongs to having dominion over a horse. Man can also use sheep. They can be shorn, and the wool can be used for making cloth. The dominion over the animals undoubtedly involves a cultural task.[37]

Man's dominion becomes even more impressive when we realize that God also gave mankind dominion over the fish of the sea and the birds of the air. They too have to serve man (after their own fashion). But in order to have dominion over fish and birds, man has to extend his influence to the sea and to the air. He has to develop the means to reach fish and birds. In other words, this dominion requires cultural development.

Much the same can be said about Genesis 1:28. Here God does not speak about man, but to him. The extent of man's government proves to be even greater than God had indicated in verse 26. At first only the dominion over the animals was mentioned, but now God says, "Fill the *earth* and subdue it." The verb meaning "to subdue" is different from that of verse 26, but it too has a negative connotation in the rest of the Bible.[38] Just like the verb meaning "to have dominion," that meaning "to subdue" can be used for making someone a slave (2 Chron. 28:10). The expression "to subdue the earth" means certainly that man has to make not only the animals, but the whole earth his servant.[39] The earth has not yet turned against man; that will happen after the Fall as a result of God's curse. But even before the Fall the earth is not automatically serving man. In Paradise man may begin to use the earth as his servant.

This dominion over the earth can be connected with the preceding words spoken to man: "Be fruitful and multiply." These words are said in a situation without sin and death. All children to be born will live and have children of their own. The two parts, dominion and having children, are interrelated. More people means the need for more of the earth to be subdued. The beginning was only a garden. But one garden will never be able to support all the people that will come; more of the earth will have to be cultivated. At the same time, more people will mean more workers to develop the earth.

One more element from verse 28 deserves mention here. "Fill the earth" and "subdue the earth" are commands given to man. Schilder spoke about a cultural mandate. *Mandate* is not a very common word, but it means nothing more than a task, a duty. It cannot be denied that such a duty was indeed given to mankind in Paradise.

The creation of man is explained in more detail in Genesis 2. After God had created man, He placed him in a garden. We should not think here of a landscaped city garden, adorned with flowers, shrubs, and grass. Without denying that flowers grew in Paradise, we have to realize that the Garden was a kind of kitchen garden. Fruit trees stood there, from which man could eat. And man had "to till." Tilling is not necessary for fruit trees; it is done in preparation for growing grain.[40] This means that even in Paradise man was not supposed to amble about, plucking fruits from the trees. The field had to be prepared for receiving the seed by plowing, the seed had to be sown, and the grain had to be harvested. Then it had to be made into flour and baked. The development of instruments for plowing, harvesting, and baking is in God's purview in His putting man in the Garden of Eden to till it. The trees were planted in the Garden to provide food for man through the cycle of sowing and harvesting, but the trees are only the beginning.[41]

Up to now we have used only texts from the period before sin entered into this world. Did this cultural mandate not change radically after the Fall? Psalm 8 shows the opposite. Man has been given dominion over the works of God's hands (v. 6). Man can rule over God's creation as Joseph ruled over Egypt (Gen. 45:8, 26). The psalm reminds us of Genesis 1. Man still has the same position in creation as he had in the beginning, sin notwithstanding.[42]

Several New Testament passages have been referred to; one is the parable of the talents in Matthew 25. We have to realize that even one talent is an enormous amount of money, more than most people at that time could ever dream of owning.[43] What do these talents signify? They cannot refer to the different abilities of the people. For it says that the servants receive their talents "each according to his ability" (v. 15). Because the slaves differ in ability, one slave receives five talents, another two, and yet another one. They have to work with the talents. The talents must therefore mean the duties given by the Lord. The Lord gives each duties according to his ability. Are these duties limited to work in the church? This is nowhere said or implied. They are all duties given by God and Jesus Christ. The duty to work in this world is certainly not excluded.[44]

Schilder also used the text "you are laborers together with God."[45] However, this text cannot support his view of culture. The reference must be to 1 Corinthians 3:9. This text reads, in the RSV, "For we are God's fellow workers; you are God's field, God's building." In this text "we" does not refer to every man, not even to every Christian, but to the ministers who preach the Word in the congregation. The congregation is called God's field, God's building.[46]

One more text can be mentioned, 1 Timothy 4:4–5. There are people who preach abstinence: no marriage, no food. Of course, the last injunction does not mean that they preach starvation. They will allow food, but it should be plain. Paul disagrees. God has created it "to be received with thanksgiving by those who believe and know the truth." Even food deliciously prepared has been created by God and may be eaten. Here we have a divine sanction for developing the gifts of the world (in this case food), if they are received with thanksgiving.[47]

Enough has been said to show that the cultural mandate has a biblical basis. There is a duty to work in this world and to develop its potential to the glory of God.

Gospel Versus Culture?

Another criticism that has been levelled against the concept of the cultural mandate is that it gives the wrong perspective on the time in which we live. The critics who make this charge do not deny that God gave a cultural mandate to man in Paradise. But they say that this duty no longer applies to our sinful world. What counts today is not cultural development but the preaching of the gospel. The Lord will return, not when the cultural mandate has been fulfilled, but when the gospel has been preached everywhere.[48]

It is true that we should not say that Christ's return depends on our fulfilling the cultural mandate. The Bible does not teach that culture must reach a certain level of development before the end of this world can come. But did Schilder say or imply that Christ's return waits for a fully developed culture? I have not been able to find this. On the contrary, Schilder strongly asserted that all the cultural effort of Christians and of those who do not believe in God will remain unfinished. Several times he used the expression "truncated pyramids" to emphasize his belief that the development of the world will remain unfinished.

But more important is the character of the period between Christ's resurrection and His return. Is this a period in which only the duty to preach has to be fulfilled, and not the duty to work in this world? If applied consistently, this opinion would imply that a Christian should work only enough to enable him and his family to live and fulfill their duties and that in all the rest of his time he has to evangelize.

Such a view clearly goes against the New Testament. For example, when John the Baptist announced the coming of the Messiah, he did not say to the tax collectors, "Give up your work, and go out and preach." He said in Luke 3:13, "Collect no more than is appointed you." And when soldiers came, he did not tell them to leave the army to become evangelists. Instead he said, "Rob no one by violence or by false accusation, and be content with your wages" (Luke 3:14). Or to give another example, the problem with Alexander (2 Tim. 4:14) was not that he was a coppersmith but that he opposed the gospel. Slaves should work faithfully as slaves. If they have the opportunity to become free men, they may do so, but it is said nowhere that then they should become (lay) preachers.

The meaning of the time between Creation and Christ's return is not limited to evangelism. It is also the period in which the Holy Spirit works in Christians to bring them to obedience to God. The Holy Spirit also requires us to see and do our daily work (as soldiers, slaves, and so on) in the light of Genesis 1 and 2, even in a world that is no longer a paradise.

It is important to maintain that in this period of the New Testament church, regeneration should become apparent in the way in which each believer fulfills his daily work. Our daily work is more than a necessity to keep us alive. Our life should show that we work as God's servants in God's world.

Cultural Mandate and Environment

The third criticism of Schilder's view of the cultural mandate is more practical. How can the cultural mandate be maintained at a time in which the dangers of developing the world have become visible? Culture has brought great progress, but this progress has happened at the expense of nature. The world is dying under the cultural mandate, it is argued. This shows all the more that we cannot use the concept of cultural mandate to define our duty in this world.[49]

It is true that nature has suffered under the use that man has made of the resources of the earth. Man did destroy part of God's creation. But how can the cultural mandate be blamed for this? Mankind began to mistreat God's creation centuries before Schilder spoke about the cultural mandate. And the misuse of creation can be found far beyond the (rather limited) circle that was influenced by Schilder's cultural mandate.

But does the cultural mandate not contribute to the idea that we can do anything we want with this world, use up all the natural resources, destroy plants and animals, and leave behind our filth? One of Schilder's expressions from *Christ and Culture* that is often referred to in this context indicates that we have to get out of the world everything we can.[50]

It would be unfair to judge Schilder on this one expression. Immediately preceding these words he gave three clear indications that destroying the earth certainly does not belong to the cultural mandate. (1) We have to develop the resources of the earth according to their individual natures. This opposes every use of creation contrary to its nature. (2) We have to develop these resources in relation to the cosmos. This implies that we may not develop one thing and at the same time destroy another. (3) We have to use the resources in obedience to God's revealed truth, the Bible. (All this is mentioned in the definition on p. 40 of *Christ and Culture*). These three restrictions show sufficiently that exploitation of God's creation is illegal.

Of course, Schilder wrote his article at a time that differed from our time. His was a time of tremendous technical and industrial progress, and only slowly the negative results have become visible. Now we are confronted with the consequences of lawless growth. We will therefore, more than Schilder could have anticipated, have to warn against the misuse of creation. We have for ourselves the duty to prevent pollution and not to leave it to the next generation to clean up our mess. But what is wrong is abnormal growth, illegal growth, dirty growth, not the use of creation itself or the development of it.

Man's way of using the world is leading to its destruction. But violation of the earth is not a part of the cultural mandate; it is the result of an egotistic dominion. The task of subduing the earth still stands.

Conclusions

If Schilder's view of a cultural mandate is in principle scriptural and correct, what are the consequences of it? I would like to point out three consequences.

1. First, we have to be aware of the broadness of our cultural work in this world. Of course, the dominion of the earth first of all

refers to the work of the farmer, the man who works in the fields. "Culture" is here very close to "cultivation." Farming is cultural work, for it is using the animal and natural resources of the world to give us food. Therefore, no one should despise the farmer.

But there is more. Schilder has a nice passage in which he applies the cultural mandate to the professor and the street sweeper, to the kitchen worker and the composer of the "Moonlight Sonata."[51] Because of the cultural mandate, our children who have the ability should be allowed to study, to become scientists, to become professors, if they can. Farmers and professors should not despise each other but should cooperate in the mandate to work in this world, each in his own place and according to his own ability.

Next, being a garbage man is not humiliating. For it is work that has to be done to keep our society going, as a part of the instruction "to keep the earth." This commandment implies keeping streets clean and preventing the outbreak of diseases.

Schilder also spoke about kitchen workers. Not many kitchen workers are left today; housewives have long taken over. With the help of electrical appliances they have to do everything themselves. Over against feminism it should be maintained that being a housewife is a good way to "subdue the earth." It is using the resources of the world to keep a family going.

And then there are those who have artistic ability. This too is a gift from God to be developed. It is true that artists often have a bad name among Christians. And the artistic world has itself partly to blame for it. They have fostered the idea that the artist must be completely free and completely himself to produce a meaningful artistic work. This often implies that the artist rejects God's Word and becomes a god to himself. When Christians reject this, they are right. On the other hand, the arts should be seen as a possibility that God has given in creation. Artists, too, should have dominion over their part of created reality.

Seen from the perspective of the cultural mandate, followers of Christ may work in many jobs. In the church no one should despise another because of the work he does. The other is a fellow worker, a servant of God in his field.[52]

2. A second result is that our daily work should be seen as part

of our obedience to God. Our jobs and work are not just means to give us enough money for our own life and for the progress of God's work in the world. Our daily job is work in the service of the Lord.

True, there is a lot of drudgery in all jobs. However, repetitive and boring work must be done as part of our daily duty before the Lord. And especially since sin has entered the world, working has not become any easier. The drudgery of our work has to be borne because we serve the Lord (again, consider the slaves). But the workers may rejoice when the harvest is in. When work is well done it brings satisfaction. This joy too is joy in the Lord. Labor Day should be a Christian celebration.

The cultural mandate gives us also the right perspective on the week. We should not drag our feet during the week from Monday to Friday and start enjoying ourselves when we can finally leave everything behind. There is a tendency today to place the emphasis on the weekend and to see the workdays as a necessary evil. Christians, however, should not live for the freedom of the weekend but work from the conviction that daily work is important in itself. It is a part of our God-given duty. That will also improve the quality of our work.[53]

3. The third consequence concerns the duty of the ministers and the elders in the church. Schilder calls Paul a cultural power in the world of his days because Paul brings the gospel of repentance and belief in Jesus Christ.[54] This gospel confronts the believers again with the duty instituted from the beginning: to have dominion over the world. God's gracious gospel puts daily jobs in the light of service to God.

Therefore, the minister cannot limit his sermon to the inner life of the believer. Daily work comes within the scope of preaching. The sermon should touch the daily life of the minister's congregation. Ethics in the workplace and in the schoolroom belongs to the things to be mentioned.

The same applies to the elder. As a matter of fact, Schilder ends his book with the elder. "Blessed is my *wise* ward elder who does his home visiting in the right way. He is a *cultural* force, although he may not be aware of it."[55] When elders visit the home, they should ask about the family's daily life before God. If the elder does his job as he should, he has to speak about God's salvation and our faith. But connected with this, he has to speak about our cultural mandate, at work, at home, and at school.

K. Schilder has been an instrument of God to teach us again the cultural mandate. We can summarize it in this way: see your daily work as part of the duty that God gave to man in the beginning; do it, as people redeemed by Jesus Christ; and work in the power of the Holy Spirit.

Notes

1. Schilder first published his views in an article entitled "Jezus Christus en het Culturele Leven" (Jesus Christ and Cultural Life). It appeared in a book with contributions from several other authors edited by N. Buffinga, *Jezus Christus en het Menschenleven* (Jesus Christ and Human Life) (Culemborg: Uitgevers-bedrijf "De Pauw," 1932), 225–85. The title of every chapter begins, "Jesus Christ and . . . ," and this is followed by the various topics: personal life, family life, church life, and so on. This gives the impression that the title of Schilder's contribution was not his own choice. The book dates from 1932, the year in which Schilder was working in Germany on his doctoral dissertation. He dictated his article to a stenographer in a few days; cf. J. J. C. Dee, *K. Schilder: Zijn Leven en Werk, Vol. 1 (1890–1934)* (Goes: Oosterbaan & Le Cointre, 1990), 245. When the second edition of *Jezus Christus en het Menschenleven* appeared, Schilder's article was left out. Schilder rewrote the article, made extensive additions, and published it separately under the title *Christus en Cultuur* (Franeker: Wever, 1948). G. van Rongen and W. Helder translated the book into English as *Christ and Culture* (Winnipeg: Premier, 1977). I shall refer to this edition.

    An interesting detail is that Schilder gave a speech on culture on December 12, 1946, in Zwolle. A summary of this speech was published, but it was not authorized by Schilder.

2. G. Puchinger published the entire discussion between Noordmans and Schilder, including Noordmans's first speech, Schilder's invitation, Noordmans's two articles, and Schilder's answer in seventeen articles, in *Een Theologie in Discussie: Over Prof. Dr. K. Schilder Profeet-Dichter-Polemist, met als Bijlage het Debat Schilder-Noordmans uit 1936* (A Theology in Discussion: Concerning Prof. Dr. K. Schilder, Prophet-Poet-Polemicist, Including the Debate Between Schilder and Noordmans in 1936) (Kampen: Kok, 1970); the quotations presented above are found on pp. 70–71, 82. Dr. Noordmans did not mince words in his original speech either: "I will not mention my final judgment on [Schilder's view of culture]. That belongs to the church. But I do want to state that I find this tone unholy, and that I never heard modernism walk so clearly on wooden shoes into the church" (p. 50). However, it is not certain that Noordmans actually uttered these harsh words in his speech. He placed this passage,

and others also, between square brackets, as if to indicate that although he thought this, he did not want to say it aloud.

When Noordmans stated that "the final judgment" on Schilder's view belongs to the church, he indicated that in his opinion the church had to deal with Schilder and should have prevented him from teaching his view. The synod of the Reformed Churches of 1936 coincided with the debate between Noordmans and Schilder. This synod decided to appoint a study committee to investigate whether certain opinions that differed from the current thoughts were acceptable in the churches. The report of this committee led to the suspension and dismissal of Schilder as professor at the seminary and as minister in the Reformed Churches, in 1944. It may well be that the remark of Noordmans about the "final judgment" sparked the ecclesiastical process against Schilder.

3. Hepp wrote four brochures under the general title *Dreigende Deformatie* (Threatening Deformation); the fourth was subtitled *De Algemeene Genade* (Common Grace) (Kampen: Kok, 1937). In this fourth brochure, as in the others, he does not mention any names. But when he writes, on p. 65, about a criticism of the doctrine of common grace that was published "in a part of a long essay, on many pages of a book and in a long series of articles in a weekly," it is obvious that he means Schilder's publications on culture. In light of the title of these brochures, it is reasonable to surmise that Hepp alluded to Schilder (among others) when he said at the synod held in 1936, "I have a few things against you, that you allow heresies," as quoted in G. Janssen, *De Feitelijke Toedracht* (The Actual Course of Events) (Groningen: Erven A. de Jager, 1955).

4. A. T. van Deursen drew attention to the seemingly general rejection of *Christ and Culture* in an article entitled "Zonde kan niet Bouwen," *Nederlands Dagblad Variant* (May 19, 1990), 3. He himself is also somewhat critical: the book has a slow start. It looks as if the writer first had to get a lot of scholarship off his chest before he really entered into his topic. Therefore, the book has a bad reputation, which it does not deserve, for it is one of Schilder's best books, says van Deursen. In the last part of this chapter we will discuss some of the recent criticisms of Schilder's views on culture.

5. The following is therefore not a review of the book *Christ and Culture*. Several theological issues that are important in the book will not be discussed here. The main question concerns what we can do with what Schilder called the cultural mandate.

6. The lectures on Calvinism were originally delivered at Princeton University, when it conferred an honorary doctor's degree on Kuyper. For this occasion Kuyper gave six special lectures on Calvinism in Princeton, in October of 1898. These lectures were published in 1899, first in English and then in Dutch. For some reactions to Kuyper's stay in the United States, see J. C. Rullmann, *Kuyper-Bibliografie*, (1891–1932) (Kampen: Kok, 1940), 3:175–80.

7. To my knowledge Kuyper first confronted culture in the last of his many series of articles in his weekly *De Heraut,* published from 1911 to 1918, between his seventy-fifth and eighty-fourth years. Because Kuyper was no longer able to

do so, his son H. H. Kuyper revised and published these articles in four volumes, under the title *Van de Voleinding* (About the Consummation) (Kampen: Kok, 1929). The passage referred to in the text can be found in vol. 2, pp. 180–81. It seems that at this time the term *culture* became popular and threatened to replace *common grace* within the Reformed community. Even though Kuyper does not absolutely reject the term *culture,* he warns against it. It is remarkable that in the rest of this book he uses it only in connection with the culture of non-Christian nations (2:172–73; 3:102–3; 4:353–54). This connection between common grace and culture is the reason why the dissertation on Kuyper's cultural views by S. J. Ridderbos, *De Theologische Cultuurbeschouwing van Abraham Kuyper* (Kampen: Kok, 1947), in fact discusses Kuyper's thoughts on common grace. This dissertation was written under the supervision of V. Hepp of the Free University.

8. The following explanation is based on A. Kuyper, *De Gemeene Gratie* (Kampen: Kok, 1932), 2:177–84. We have omitted what Kuyper says about the development of Arabian culture.

9. This part of our discussion shows that Kuyper sees a relation between Christ as Head of the world and the progress of common grace. He therefore returns to common grace in his book about Christ entitled *Pro Rege: Of het Koningschap van Christus* (For the King: About the Kingship of Christ) (Kampen: Kok, 1911), 3:261–62.

10. Ibid., 183.

11. Also in his lectures on Calvinism, Kuyper explains his views on the stunted development of cultures that receive only common grace, over against the continuous development of Western culture under the influence of special grace. He compares the other cultures with stagnant pools and Western culture with a continuous river that makes growth possible; see A. Kuyper, *Lectures on Calvinism* (Grand Rapids: Eerdmans, 1970 [reprint]), 32; the same example occurs in Kuyper, *De Gemeene Gratie,* 2:670–74. The views of Kuyper on culture are explained in the doctoral dissertation of S. J. Ridderbos cited in note 7 above; in J. Douma, *Algemene Genade: Uiteenzetting, Vergelijking en Beoordeling van de Opvattingen van A. Kuyper, K. Schilder en J. Calvijn over 'Algemene Genade'* (Goes: Oosterbaan & Le Cointre, 1966), a doctoral dissertation at the Theological University in Kampen (Broederweg); and in H. R. Van Til, *The Calvinist Concept of Culture* (Philadelphia: Presbyterian and Reformed, 1972). E. E. Ericson, Jr., "Abraham Kuyper: Cultural Critic," *Calvin Theological Journal* 22, no. 2 (1987), concentrates on a different aspect of Kuyper. It is indeed remarkable that much of Western culture, especially its technology, has been accepted by countries with a different cultural background. It is questionable, however, whether the development of Western culture can be explained as the result of the influence of Christianity. M. J. Paul states that the high levels of scholarship and technical science in Western culture can also be the result of the Renaissance and humanism in a lecture entitled "Cultuurmandaat en Vreemdelingschap," reported in *Nederlands Dagblad* (September 7, 1989),

2; see also J. Douma, "Christus en Cultuur," in J. Douma and C. Trimp, eds., *K. Schilder: Aspecten van zijn Werk* (Barneveld: Vuurbaak, 1990), 191.

12. See also the admiration expressed by A. A. van Ruler in Douma, *Algemene Genade,* 50.

13. This does not mean that the development of Kuyper's view of common grace precedes the founding of the party and of the university. The party was founded in 1879 and the Free University in 1880, while he really started using the concept of common grace in 1887 and wrote his books on common grace between 1895 and 1901 (cf. Douma, *Algemene Genade,* 90–91). Of course, Kuyper had his reasons for founding the party and the university. But the all-encompassing context developed slowly and rather late. This is not uncommon for Kuyper. He gave the full reasons for the theological department of his Free University, which was among the first departments (1880), long afterwards in his *Encyclopaedie der Heilige Godgeleerdheid* (Kampen: Kok, 1894). See also what he wrote to H. Bavinck, as quoted in R. H. Bremmer, *Herman Bavinck en zijn Tijdgenoten* (Kampen: Kok, 1966), 81.

14. In 1918 (when the First World War ended) O. Spengler began to publish his *Untergang des Abendlandes,* about the downfall of Europe. According to him, European civilization was past its zenith and in decline. Later E. Maria Remarque wrote his novel *Im Westen nichts Neues* (1929) in which he wanted to show that Western society had destroyed all values without offering new ones. In an interesting article, "Hoe Vernieuwend was Schilder?" *Nederlands Dagblad Variant* (September 21, 1990), 35, G. Harinck points to these facts to explain why Schilder does not have high hopes when he speaks about culture. Schilder does not mention beauty in connection with culture but speaks of rubber boots and tears. No doubt Schilder was less optimistic about Western civilization than Kuyper (even though Kuyper too began to have his doubts [Kuyper, *Gemeene Gratie,* 2:183]). However, Schilder does speak of beauty in connection with culture (cf. the "composer of a Moonlight Sonata" [Schilder, *Christ and Culture,* 39]). On the same page the rubber boots are mentioned, but not as an example of the difficulty of cultural work; rather, they are mentioned as something that had to be invented as part of the cultural work. Harinck seems to try to explain Schilder's view from the historical setting. Schilder would have objected to this. He wanted to speak within his own time, to be sure, but on the basis of Scripture. His main difference from Kuyper is in his use of Scripture, not in his cultural outlook.

15. Schilder, *Christ and Culture,* 27.

16. Ibid., 35. It may appear as if Schilder is speaking only about the New Testament church, but that would be a misunderstanding. Of course Schilder recognizes that Jesus Christ came "in the fullness of time." But he takes into account the fact that Jesus Christ is the eternal Son of God and that He already was appointed Savior before His birth on earth. Also during the period of the Old Testament He did His saving work, "because He as the Messiah, even before appearing under the name of Jesus, and also afterwards—that is, all through

the centuries—takes action by virtue of the *right* to be obtained or already obtained in the middle of history, by His redeeming *power,* He makes certain people again as they were 'in the beginning': men of God" (*Christ and Culture,* 35). Schilder emphasizes the importance of Christ's office in order to escape the dangers of an "exemplaric" use of the name *Jesus Christ.* This means that Schilder does not want to derive the Christian view of culture from the *details* of Christ's life, such as the gold, incense, and myrrh that He received after His birth; the rich women who served Him; the woman who anointed Him; His expensive garment; and so on (*Christ and Culture,* 23, 28–29). Not the details of His life, but His function as Savior should determine the Christian view of culture. Schilder's article titled "Jesus Christ and Cultural Life" should be seen against the background of the three volumes he wrote under the title *Christ in His Suffering,* trans. H. Zylstra (Grand Rapids: Eerdmans, 1938) in 1930—two years prior to the article on culture. In these books Schilder showed that Christ's work in His suffering should not be seen as an example for us, but as His saving work for us. In the article on culture Schilder worked out this conviction with regard to a particular topic. See on this J. Kamphuis, "Vormingswerk Onder een Open Hemel III," *De Reformatie* 62, no. 25 (1987): 505–6.

17. This is the first difference between Kuyper and Schilder on the issue of culture, and it is the fundamental one. But Schilder in writing his article seems not to have been aware of this different starting point. In the original 1932 article the only criticism of Kuyper (without mention of his name) is that it will not do to discuss culture as a matter of common grace (Buffinga, *Jezus Christus en het Menschenleven,* 277).

18. Van Til, in *The Calvinist Concept of Culture,* approaches Schilder's view of culture from the perspective of Schilder's *What Is Heaven?* As a result, he makes statements like the following: "Schilder would evaluate the cultural process on the basis of its eschatological-pedagogical worth" (p. 148). This is a misrepresentation, however. Not only did the book on heaven appear three years later than the publication on culture, but Schilder nowhere evaluates culture on the basis of eschatology; in contrast, he evaluates it consistently on the basis of protology.

19. Schilder, *Christ and Culture,* 44.

20. Ibid., 53.

21. Here is the second difference between Kuyper and Schilder concerning culture. Kuyper takes his starting point in the world of sin. Then he is amazed that so much cultural development is still possible. The explanation must be that it is the result of common grace. Schilder begins earlier in time, with the commands that God gave in Paradise. These commands of Paradise show what culture should be.

22. Schilder, *Christ and Culture,* 40.

23. The word *culture* has many meanings. "Hundreds of definitions exist," according to T. Hard, *Culture and Conviction: Culture, the Mark and Measure of*

Conviction in Religious Community (Pusan, South Korea: Kosin College and Korea Theological Seminary, 1983), 11. The meaning that Schilder gives to the word is not the common Dutch usage, as can be seen in the Dutch dictionary by Van Dale. It is also not the meaning of culture given by F. W. Grosheide in the contemporary *Christelijke Encyclopaedie,* vol. 1 (Kampen: Kok, 1925), 526–28. Here culture is taken to mean civilization. The publishers of the book *Jesus Christus en het Menschenleven* probably did not expect Schilder to write on man's work in the world in general when they asked him to write on "Jesus Christ and cultural life." The other chapters have titles such as "Jesus Christ and Church Life," "Jesus Christ and Political Life," and "Jesus Christ and Social Life." Under the title "Jesus Christ and Cultural Life" they might have expected an article concentrating on the arts. Schilder was suited to that task. He probably knew more about culture in that sense than any other minister in the Reformed churches at that time. He knew literature and had written about the theater in "Onze Verhouding tot het Tooneel," *Opgang* 8, no. 3a (1924): 69–80. It is possible that Schilder derived the meaning he gave to *culture* from H. Bavinck. In a chapter about revelation and culture Bavinck, in H. Bavinck,*Wijsbegeerte der Openbaring. Stone Lectures* (Kampen: Kok, 1908), gives the following description: "Culture in the broadest sense of the word includes all the work which human powers bestow on nature" (p. 213).

24. Schilder, *Christ and Culture,* 37.

25. J. Douma, "Christus en Cultuur," 188, states that Schilder used the word *culture* in three different senses: (1) the comprehensive sense, in which culture includes everything, from agriculture to worship; (2) the more common and limited sense, which includes technical and artistic work; and (3) *culture* as the presupposition for the fulfillment of God's blessing and God's curse. I cannot agree with Douma here. This third sense is not of the same nature as the first and the second. It does not say what culture is but what it is for. It is true that Schilder speaks of culture in connection with a double destination, but that does not make this a sense. Concerning the second sense, no reference given by Douma proves that *culture* was used in the book in the sense of technical and artistic work. For example, one quotation is taken from the page (p. 40 in the English translation) on which Schilder gives his extensive definition of culture. The quotation is as follows: "The garden is the beginning of *adama,* of the inhabited world. Hence it is also the beginning of the cultural world." Schilder is here speaking about "cultural life and all its processes," not just about subjects like technical work and the arts. I also beg to disagree with the first sense that Douma gives. As far as I can see, *culture* is indeed consistently used by Schilder in a comprehensive sense, but it never includes worship. Schilder attacks the separation of culture and religion, for example, on p. 42, but he does not identify culture and religion. Schilder arrived at this comprehensive sense on the basis of texts like Gen. 1:28 and 2:15.

26. Schilder, *Christ and Culture,* 39. When Schilder speaks of evolution on the basis of creation, he does not distinguish between Gen. 1:1 and the rest of chap.

1, but between Gen. 1:1–2:9 and 2:15–17. In other words, creation does not include only the first creation of God, but the work of creation of all six days. Evolution includes here the work that man does in God's world.

27. Ibid., 39–40.

28. Schilder's view of the cultural mandate has been developed for application to technical science by J. R. Wiskerke, "Schriftuurlijke Taxatie van de Techniek," *Lucerna* 8, nos. 1, 2 (1969): 13–23.

29. Schilder, *Christ and Culture*, 62.

30. Ibid., 63.

31. Ibid., 70.

32. Ibid., 71. Here the third major difference between Kuyper and Schilder becomes visible. According to Kuyper, there cannot and should not be a Christian culture. For Christ adds his particular grace to the culture of Greece and Rome as a result of common grace. Therefore, Christians should not try to make a specific Christian culture. They should further Christianize Western culture. Schilder says that there should be Christian culture, in distinction from the work of unbelievers. For Christ regenerates people to renewed obedience to the original mandate. The result will be a Christian culture.

Schilder therefore also has to discuss the question of whether Christians and non-Christians can cooperate; see paragraph 20 of *Christ and Culture*. We cannot go into a discussion of this point, but we have to note that problems arise here. Schilder is building on the "antithesis" idea of Kuyper. But can the work of Christians be so sharply separated from the work of others as Schilder tries to make it? To use his own expression, do they build different pyramids? Are they not often cooperating in building the same pyramid, but from a different conviction? Of course, the difference in conviction should come out in the attitude, but it becomes only partially visible in the results of their work. Faith does not usually lead to a completely different result. See also Douma, "Christus en Cultuur," 190–91, where the example is given of the two women of Matt. 24:40, who cooperate in the same cultural work even though one believes while the other does not.

33. Schilder, *Christ and Culture*, 60.

34. Ibid., 43.

35. The fourth difference from the view of Kuyper is that Kuyper explained culture as a result of common grace and Schilder replaced the grace with a mandate. Schilder showed already in the article of 1932 that he could not agree with common grace (pp. 277–78). This criticism became much stronger in the book edition of 1947 (pp. 71–74). The fact that Kuyper saw culture more as the result, while Schilder saw it more as the work, is connected with this difference in approach.

Schilder's rejection of common grace gave rise to one of the greatest debates surrounding Schilder's view of culture. One of the debated topics was the character of the time after the fall into sin. Is the fact that time and life continue and that progress is possible in the fallen world not a result of common grace?

No is the answer of Schilder. For time in itself is not grace. Some people use their time wisely, in the service of God. But many do not make good use of the time and the opportunities that they have. They will be condemned because of the way in which they use the time. Schilder therefore called time the *substratum,* the underlying ground for blessing and curse (p. 47). Douma has criticized Schilder. He does not defend Kuyper's view of common grace but wants to return to the less grand view of common grace held by Calvin. In my opinion Douma is correct when he criticizes the neutral way in which time and the benefits of God's earth are presented by Schilder (Douma, *Algemene Genade,* 310–11, 320–23). However, can the term *grace* be used in connection with time? It seems to me that all the opportunities that time gives and all the abilities that humanity receives are gifts from God's goodness more than results of God's grace. Since this difference, however, does not directly bear on the discussion of the cultural mandate, we need not discuss it in detail here.

36. J. Douma questioned whether the biblical passages give the right to speak of a cultural mandate (Douma, *Algemene Genade,* 345). J. Kamphuis criticized Douma's exegesis in articles devoted to Douma's dissertation in his *Onderweg Aangesproken: Beschouwingen over Kerk, Confessie en Cultuur* (Groningen: De Vuurbaak, 1968), 228–44. As a result Douma softened his criticism in a speech later added to his dissertation (374–78). The discussion began again with an article by F. Pansier, "Cultuurmandaat: Vastigheid of Zeepbel?" *Radix* 15, no. 3 (1989): 124–34. Douma answered this in "Is het Cultuurmandaat een Zeepbel?" *Nederlands Dagblad Variant* (September 16, 1989), 3. M. J. Paul joined the critics in a speech in which he discussed the question of whether Christians have a cultural mandate or whether they are sojourners on earth. His conclusion from a discussion of the texts in Gen. 1 and 2 is as follows: "From the analysis of these texts it appears that God allows the use of the fruits of the garden and of the earth. But the most important thing is that it says nowhere that man has the mandate to establish a culture. To a certain extent we may use the culture around us" (*Nederlands Dagblad Variant* [September 7, 1989], 2).

37. Schilder connected the dominion of man with his being created "in the image of God." For his discussion see K. Schilder, *Heidelbergsche Catechismus,* 4 vols. (Goes: Oosterbaan & Le Cointre, 1947–51), 1:220–312. J. Kamphuis developed this idea in J. Kamphuis, *Uit Verlies Winst: Het Beeld van God en het Komende Koninkrijk* (Barneveld: Vuurbaak, 1985), and in Kamphuis, "Vormingswerk Onder een Open Hemel."

38. A. van Selms, *Genesis I* (Nijkerk: Callenbach, 1973), 36, 38–39, gives special attention to the violent character of the verbs meaning "to have dominion" and "to subdue." This brings him to the question Is the universe friendly? In his answer he remarks that God, who created the universe, is friendly. It belongs to God's friendliness towards us that He has given us the difficult duty to make the earth subservient to us, but the earth resists and has to be subdued violently. The emphasis on hard work is in my opinion correct, but the idea of a resisting earth does not fit Gen. 1.

39. Pansier, "Cultuurmandaat," 125, makes the remark that *earth* has several meanings in the Bible: land, a part of the land region, the territory of a nation, the earth as that part of the world where man and animals live (over against sea and sky), and the inhabitants of a country. He notes the fact that the verb *to subdue* in connection with *the earth* means "to subdue the inhabitants of a nation." According to him, we have to take the words in the meaning they have in other passages too and not invent new meanings for them. The meaning of the last remark is not clear. Does Pansier mean that we have to take *earth* in the last sense, since "to subdue the earth" is a common combination in the Bible? This is obviously impossible here, for it would mean that God told the ancestor of all mankind to subdue all future generations. However, we need not invent a new sense for *earth;* the meaning is that which already occurred in this chapter: the created world, the earth in which we live (Gen. 1:1–2). This sense brings us right back to the cultural mandate.

40. The verb meaning "to till" includes all the work of agriculture that must be performed in order for people to eat (cf. Gen. 3:18–19). The verb occurs in connection with the products of the land and bread in 2 Sam. 9:10–11. Oxen and asses may be used for it (Isa. 30:24; Deut. 15:19) (again, domesticating animals belongs to "cultural" work). "Tilling" is also done to a vineyard (Deut. 28:39).

 God not only said that man had to till, but also that he had to "keep" the Garden. This supposes that the Garden is threatened. W. Gispen, *Genesis I, Commentaar Oude Testament* (Kampen: Kok, 1974), 121, thinks the threat comes from Satan. More probable is the opinion of van Selms, that the animals are meant (van Selms, *Genesis I,* 55).

41. Because of all this I cannot agree with the conclusion of M. J. Paul that the Bible nowhere says that man has a mandate to establish a culture (see note 36 above).

 It is too remarkable not to mention that Gen. 2 also speaks about gold and precious stones in the countries surrounding Paradise. In the context this remark cannot serve to identify the countries; they are sufficiently identified by their names. In the mentioning of gold and precious stones it is implied that man was to venture out of the Garden, discover the gold and the precious stones, and use them for decoration. See for this also J. Kapteyn, *Van Hem, Die is Die was en Die Komt* (Goes: Oosterbaan & Le Cointre, n.d.), 37, and N. Gootjes, "Some Thoughts on Rivers of Paradise," *Clarion* 40, nos. 23, 24 (1991): 491–93, 512–14.

42. Cf. N. H. Ridderbos, *De Psalmen* (Kampen: Kok, 1962), 1:117–18. He says that Ps. 8 reminds us of Gen. 1. The difference is that according to Gen. 1 it was man's destination to govern in the recently created world. Ps. 8 says that the same applies to the world as we know it, the world that has been destroyed by sin. According to Ridderbos (p. 123), we cannot limit man's dominion in Ps. 8 to dominion over the animals. The fact that man reigns over the birds and the fish also implies that the sky and the sea are not excepted from the dominion of man.

Gen. 3:17–19 can also be mentioned in this connection. Man's work on the earth becomes difficult and painful, but the duty given in the beginning is maintained by God; cf. J. Francke, *Lichtende Verbintenissen* (Kampen: van den Berg, 1985), 36.

43. Therefore, this parable has to be distinguished from the parable of the pounds in Luke 19. For a pound is only a small amount of money.

44. One of the criticisms that M. J. Paul has brought against the cultural mandate is that the parable of Matt. 25 does not speak of work in general, but of spiritual work, the work in the kingdom of God. However, the kingdom cannot be limited to "spiritual" work, to the exclusion of work in general. When Jesus Christ before his ascension told his followers to make disciples of all nations, He told them in Matt. 28:19 to teach them "to observe *all* that I have commanded you." Jesus' teaching of the kingdom was never limited to works such as evangelism, preaching, and missions. It included obedience to God in daily life, as also the Sermon on the Mount shows. The merchant had to be honest and not sell his goods by means of big oaths. A limitation of the talents to spiritual work, as Dr. Paul proposes, is not indicated in Matt. 25, and it is contradicted in the gospel of Matthew. If there is a limitation indicated, then it is not in the talents, but in the servants. They are the servants of Christ, which implies that members of the church are meant (cf. note 36 above).

45. Schilder, *Christ and Culture,* 39.

46. In the Dutch edition *Christus en Cultuur* (p. 53), Schilder does not indicate which text he quotes. That he has a text in mind is clear, however, for he says, "This is not only a suitable text for a minister's inaugural sermon, but is also the day-text for any cultural worker" (p. 39). The word for "fellow workman" occurs only a few times in the New Testament, and it is used only twice in connection with God, in 1 Cor. 3:9 and 1 Thess. 3:2 (but in the latter text the manuscripts give different readings). The only possible identification of the quotation is therefore 1 Cor. 3:9. But at the time of Schilder's writing, the text "You are laborers together with God" was probably a standard expression. It was used as the title of a book containing many practical remarks about jobs, marriage, and life in society by D. van Dijk, *Gij zijt Gods Medearbeiders* (You are God's Fellow Workers) (Goes: Oosterbaan & Le Cointre, 1942).

47. We can in this connection also think of texts such as Ps. 24:1, "The earth is the Lord's and the fulness thereof," and Ps. 104:14–15, "Thou dost cause the grass to grow for the cattle, and plants for man to cultivate, that he may bring forth food from the earth, and wine to gladden the heart of man, oil to make his face shine, and bread to strengthen man's heart." Plants grow under God's providence for man to make wine and oil. But a considerable amount of "cultural development" goes into making wine and oil.

48. This criticism can be found especially in W. H. Velema, *Ethiek en Pelgrimage* (Amsterdam: Ton Bolland, 1974), chap. 5, "Cultuurmandaat en Vreemdelingschap." Velema recently repeated this criticism in a lecture on Schilder (*Nederlands Dagblad* [February 7, 1990], 2), and in an article in *De Waarheidsvriend*

(*Nederlands Dagblad* [August 27, 1990], 2). Velema is here, according to Kamphuis, "Vormingswerk Onder een Open Hemel," 507, under the influence of G. C. Berkouwer, and so indirectly under the influence of K. Barth.

49. One of the reasons why M. J. Paul studied the cultural mandate was an interest in the environment that exists today: "Christians are being accused that they have dominated the earth and the animals" (*Nederlands Dagblad* [September 7, 1989], 2). The environment was also the theme at the annual "school day" in 1989 of the theological college in Kampen. J. Douma (*Nederlands Dagblad* [September 14, 1989], 2) defended speaking about the cultural mandate with regard to the crisis concerning the environment. He argued that we need not be afraid to speak of "having dominion" and of "developing creation" or to use the expression "cultural mandate." For these words show that we are stewards and that we therefore are answerable to God for our use of the environment.

Another critic is W. H. Velema, *Nederlands Dagblad* (February 17, 1990), 2; one of the reasons for his objection to the totalitarian and programmatic character of Schilder's view of the cultural mandate is that it can no longer be defended in light of today's ecological crisis. Velema has been answered by J. de Vos, "Cultural Mandate and Environment," in *Reformed Perspective* 9, no. 7 (1990): 16–19.

A different proposal came from J. Huijgen in "Van Cultuurmandaat naar Natuurmandaat?" *Beweging* 54, no. 4 (1990): 67–68, and it was repeated in a speech at a congress for the "Stichting voor Reformatorische Wijsbegeerte" (*Nederlands Dagblad* [October 16, 1990], 2). Culture is destroying nature, according to Huijgen. Therefore, we have to develop a natural mandate next to the cultural mandate, to give an independent place to nature. Douma has given a critical evaluation of this proposal in J. Douma, "Natuurmandaat naast Cultuurmandaat?" *Nederlands Dagblad Variant* (September 29, 1990), 5.

50. The Dutch has here "Uit de wereld halen wat erin zit" (Schilder, *Christus en Cultuur,* 55). The English translation reads, "To exploit the world's potentials" (*Christ and Culture,* 40).

51. Schilder, *Christ and Culture,* 39.

52. This does not mean, of course, that Christians can work in just any job. A shocking illustration of this was once given by Dr. S. Greijdanus. He made the remark that something is not automatically good when we add the word *Christian* to it. For that would mean that we could have Christian brothels.

Limitations exist also on a personal basis. We sometimes have to limit ourselves because of the kingdom. A minister with artistic ability can be so busy in his congregation that he has no time to develop his gift. A housewife who has to take care of her children will not have much time left for many other things that she has the ability to do. Self-development can never be the ultimate goal.

M. J. Paul asked the critical question of whether biotechnology and genetic manipulation can be developed without limitation as part of the cultural mandate; see *Nederlands Dagblad* (September 7, 1989), 2. But this in itself cannot be brought against the cultural mandate, because this mandate implies obedience to God. See for a careful weighing of this question with regard to the field of medical research J. A. Los, "De Kwetsbaarheid van de Christen in de Wetenschap," *Radix* 16, no. 3 (1990): 100–117.

53. The harvest feasts in the Old Testament remind us of the joy in completed work under the blessing of the Lord. There were even three feasts, each of which was celebrated after a part of the harvest was in. They were to be celebrated with great joy; cf. Lev. 23:9–44; Deut. 16:9–17. In this connection it should be noted that having no occupation during the days of the week does not come easily to mankind. This underlines the fact that working forms an integral part of man's existence in this world.

54. Schilder, *Christ and Culture,* 49–50.

55. Ibid., 86.

4

SCHILDER ON THE CHURCH

J. M. Batteau

Klaas Schilder's emphasis on the importance of the church remains one of the most striking aspects of his work as a pastor, a journalist, and a professor of dogmatics.[1] Although he never wrote a thorough dogmatic treatment of this subject, we can glean his basic concepts from his multitudinous writings, both popular and scholarly. His convictions in this area that contributed to the Liberation (*Vrijmaking*) of 1944 were contested by other theologians and are still a source of conflict in the Dutch and international theological scenes today. Schilder is accused of "absolutizing" the visible church, and he is even charged with having sectarian notions.[2] But are such accusations valid? Does Schilder stand outside the mainstream of the Reformed tradition? Or can his thoughts rather be a real stimulus for us to seek biblical and Reformed church unity?

In a recent article on Schilder's ecclesiology in a volume celebrating the one hundredth year of his birth, H. J. D. Smit, a minister of the Reformed Churches (Liberated),[3] characterizes Schilder's concept of the church as one stressing the absolute call of God to membership in the true church.[4] Schilder asserts that believers who are not members of true churches maintaining scriptural unity are fundamentally disobedient to God and cannot claim God's blessing in their church life. Smit recognizes the radical nature of this view and appreciates its biblical forcefulness, but he wonders if it does justice to the complexity and stubbornness of sin after the Fall; he cites the Heidelberg Catechism, Lord's Day 44: "But can those converted to God keep these commandments perfectly?" "No. In this life even the holiest have only a small beginning of this obedience. . . ." Smit finds in this exposition grounds for criticizing Schilder's radical expectation that all believers be members of united, truly Reformed churches.[5] To say that God commands all believers to be members of such churches is one thing. To demand visible church unity as an absolute prerequisite to fellowship and cooperation is another.

We see here that even within the Reformed Churches (Liberated) of the present day an animated discussion continues about Schilder's views regarding the church.[6] His ideas in this area remain stimulating and continue to evoke a wide-ranging variety of responses.[7] This shows the continuing vitality and challenge of his concepts.

To give a thorough exposition of Schilder's ecclesiology would demand more space than can be given to one chapter in a volume of this sort. What follows is an attempt to focus on certain central issues in Schilder's thinking about the church. Smit's approach is undoubtedly a valid one: singling out certain key concepts (he mentions obedience to God's demand; the church "in movement" in history; the centrality of the covenant; criticism of Abraham Kuyper, Sr.; and the revaluing of the Belgic Confession on the church) in order to delineate Schilder's basic position. I have, however, chosen a somewhat different approach. By discussing various continuities and discontinuities that Schilder's ecclesiology demonstrates, both in his own theological development and in relation to the Reformed theological tradition as a whole, I hope to be able to illuminate Schilder's thinking about the church.

Continuity and Discontinuity: Schilder Himself

It is not difficult to signal certain developments in Schilder's approach to the subject of the church over the course of his life.[8] A student of the dogmatician A. G. Honig in Kampen, who was in turn indebted to both Abraham Kuyper, Sr., and Herman Bavinck,[9] Schilder in his preaching and writing on the church from 1910 to 1930 reflected the existing consensus of the theological faculties of the Reformed Churches at the Free University of Amsterdam and at the seminary in Kampen. Typical is Schilder's appeal to "Dort, Kuyper, and Bavinck" in his criticism of J. J. Buskes in 1928.[10] Schilder wanted at that time nothing other than to continue the struggle that the Synod of 1618–19 and those two great Dutch theologians represented. This was true with respect to the authority of Scripture, the key issue at the Synod of Assen in 1926, and it was also true with respect to ecclesiology. Smit can legitimately claim that until 1934 it was as though Schilder echoed Kuyper on the theme of the invisible church.[11]

Even at the beginning of the 1930s, however, Schilder had begun to question Kuyper's theory of the pluriformity of the church.[12] As the 1930s progressed, Schilder began more pointedly to question various concepts of Kuyper's, including the "invisible church" theory. And by the time of the synodical discussions at the beginning of the 1940s, Schilder was openly critical of Kuyper's ecclesiology as a whole.[13] In Schilder's ecclesiology is thus evident the development of a supporter (in general terms) of Kuyper's theology and ecclesiology into an opponent on many important points. A similar development is traceable with regard to Schilder's theology of the covenant.[14]

But before we trace these differences, the discontinuities in Schilder's own ecclesiological development, in more detail, let us first look at some of the basic continuities.

Continuity: the Authority of Scripture and the Church

A Church of the Word. Schilder was for his whole life an orthodox Reformed theologian who upheld the inspiration and infallibility of the Bible and its freedom from genuine contradictions. He wrote a typically Schilderian booklet in 1919, "popular" yet very scholarly, with much documentation, about the alleged discrepancies in the Bible, in which he could say that there are indeed discrepancies in the Bible in the form in which we now have it. However, he writes, "We Reformed people do *not* accept that in the *original* manuscripts those errors existed."[15]

In this work Schilder criticizes not only liberal modernism, which freely used higher criticism in its approach to the Bible, but also "ethical" theology, which was moderate in its criticism but nevertheless saw room for contradictions and errors in the Bible. Schilder rejects this approach, asserting instead that some apparent contradictions in Scripture as we now have it are the result of copying errors. Through *textual* criticism we have the weapons to defeat (higher) *Scripture* criticism.[16] Other apparent contradictions regarding God's thoughts and behavior are simply anthropomorphisms. Further, certain problems of harmonization remain, but in many cases we can see possible good solutions for the supposed contradictions, and we may continue to have confidence that God's Word is infallible. If our starting point, the inspiration and unity of the entire Bible, is sound, we have a "nonscientific" but nevertheless firm presuppositional basis upon which to investigate the Bible itself. And all men begin with presuppositions (*vooroordeelen*).[17]

This high view of Scripture remained a permanent fixture of Schilder's faith-convictions and theology.[18] During the two major crises of the Reformed Churches in the 1920s, the confirmation of the condemnation of J. B. Netelenbos by the Synod of Leeuwarden in 1920 and the suspension and consequent removal of J. G. Geelkerken as a minister in 1926 by the Synod of Assen, Schilder stood firmly behind the synods. He repeatedly defended the historicity of the biblical account of the Fall over against Geelkerken and the so-called Hersteld Verband churches in 1926 and in following years.[19] And in the 1930s and 1940s, Schilder maintained a constant critique of Karl Barth and the Dutch Barthians, who saw room for historical and even "dogmatic" error in Scripture. Schilder was sharpest in his rejection of an orthodox-sounding theology that in fact refused to bow before God's authority in His written Word.[20] This criticism was nothing new for Schilder but a continuation of a polemic that he had carried on for years.

In Schilder's view, bowing to Scripture was not just a demand for individual believers, but a necessity for the true church of Christ. Schilder saw the church as a church under the authority of Scripture, and characterized by loyalty to Scripture.[21] In this he was simply but forcefully echoing the Belgic Confession, which calls the Holy Scriptures an "infallible rule" (original text: *reigle infallible*)[22] in article 7 and which names the "pure preaching of the gospel" as one of the three marks of the true church (article 29), along with "the pure administration of the sacraments" and "Church discipline." Where loyalty to God's Word was undermined or unclear, there a church had ceased to be a biblical church. Schilder emphasizes this in his polemical exchanges with theologians from the Dutch Reformed Church in the 1930s and 1940s.[23] To the rise of the ecumenical movement, which culminated with the establishment of the World Council of Churches in 1948, Schilder responded by pointing out the movement's lack of scriptural foundation, that of the apostles and prophets.[24] Where this foundation is not present, there can be no true church. For Schilder, ecclesiology flows directly from one's view of the Bible.

A Word About the Church. Schilder not only confessed his allegiance to Scripture, calling the church to loyalty to Scripture, but from the first he also continually sought to sound the depths of the divine revelation in order to understand *better* what God had revealed with regard to the church.[25] A constant element in his theology is a searching of the Scriptures for more wisdom from God. While holding wholeheartedly to the Dutch Reformed confessions (the Belgic Confession, the Heidelberg Catechism, and the Canons of Dort), he was no mere confessionalist, content to parrot the statements of the confessions, but sought new light in God's Word through exegesis and always attempted to relate one part of Scripture to others, sometimes doing so in surprising new ways.[26]

We see this appeal to Scripture as the basic standard, combined with new insights derived from Scripture and attention to the challenges and dangers of the modern world, in sermons and Bible meditations throughout his life. In a 1918 sermon on the topic "Judgment begins with the house of God" (1 Pet. 4:17), Schilder describes in light of the Scripture text how the church, although a city on a hill and God's house, must *first* undergo God's judgment. Sin in *her* midst is to Him a *greater abomination* than sin in the world. That is why He lets His judgment come first to the congregation. The church is not automatically free from judgment, just as God's people in Ezekiel 9 were not free from judgment.[27] Here we see Schilder basing his message on Scripture, as a unity of the Old and New Testaments, and bringing the bright light of God's Word to bear on the real dangers of his day, in this case the tendency of church members to be nonchalant and to make light of God's judgment. The church can never rest on her laurels, but she must be confronted continually with God's high demands.

In a meditation written in 1949 on Luke 6:13 (". . . and chose from them twelve, whom he named apostles . . ."), Schilder refers to the following Scripture passages: Hebrews 2:13; Psalm 22; Psalm 18; 2 Samuel 21 and 22; Isaiah 8; and John 1, 16, and 17. He calls Christ a "father" who chooses "sons," the twelve apostles.

> . . . *Pater ecclesiae,* spiritual father of the church, which He gathers through the twelve who lead in the service of the Word. Because the entire fellowship of the new covenant will be built upon their teaching as foundation. Twelve patriarchs "displayed" once the entire church; twelve apostles shall from now on display her: twelve "vocations" through the Word, through which the pupils-sons will from now on follow their "father-brother." They are the *toledoth,* the decisive genesis of the new Testament.[28]

Here we see a typical Schilderian manner of reflecting on Scripture, the New Testament building upon and fulfilling the Old. The church is Christ's church, built on the apostles, as revealed in this one Word of divine revelation.

Schilder's ecclesiology was thus fundamentally built on Scripture and continually oriented to Scripture. Here the Protestant adage of *Sola Scriptura* was maintained, without a mere repetition of past Reformed positions and standard interpretations. For Schilder, Scripture always had the first and last word. He was bound to the text, but because he was bound, he had freedom, even the solemn responsibility, to listen anew and to seek new vistas in God's truth. This seeking to listen anew to the voice of God in the Word characterizes Schilder's entire life. From the beginning of his work as a pastor he eschewed conservatism and sought originality of insight and expression. This gives his sermons and writings on the church a freshness and a vibrancy often lacking in the work of his contemporaries, who may have been just as orthodox but who tended merely to want to conserve, rather than to reform and renew.

CONTINUITY: GOD'S CALL TO CHURCH UNITY

Another constant factor in Schilder's writing about the church is his call to church unity based on Scripture and the Reformed confessions. The closest separate church group to the Reformed Churches was the Christelijke Gereformeerde Church ("Christian Reformed" Church), made up of those local churches of the Secession (*Afscheiding*) of 1834 that refused to go along with the union with the *Doleantie* churches[29] in 1892.[30] It was only natural that Schilder focused on calling these churches to unite with the Reformed Churches. Because the Christelijke Gereformeerde Church wanted to stay apart from the union, Schilder saw it as schismatic. In his view, Reformed believers had needlessly isolated themselves from the union of 1892, without sufficient biblical or confessional warrant.

During the 1920s, early in his career as a journalist, Schilder wrote extensively, in the weeklies *De Bazuin* and *De Reformatie,* about what he regarded as the errors of various Christelijke Gereformeerde spokesmen. Several issues continually reappear. One was the question of Abraham Kuyper's Reformed orthodoxy. And closely related to this issue was the matter of the doctrine of regeneration, with regard to which the Christelijke Gereformeerde leaders dismissed Abraham Kuyper as a "neo-Reformed" theologian.

Schilder says repeatedly in *De Bazuin* that the critique of Kuyper by Christelijke Gereformeerde theologians is unfounded and unfair.[31] While the latter maintain that Kuyper taught "presumed regeneration," to the effect that all children of believers are believed to be already regenerate, Schilder responds by saying that since the statement of the Synod of 1905 regarding regeneration and baptism, the official teaching of the Reformed Churches has been quite different. *Regarding* children of believers as regenerate (the language of the 1905 declaration) is totally different from saying that all such children *are* in fact regenerate. When the Christelijke Gereformeerde lecturer from Apeldoorn, van der Schuit, accuses Kuyper of teaching a "slumbering" regeneration, so that believers are "unconscious" of their being regenerate, Schilder responds by saying that Kuyper merely taught the *possibility* of such a situation, which van der Schuit himself admitted in theory.

In these polemics we notice how Schilder reasons about the church. First, he emphasizes the broadness of the church,[32] with room for Kuyper and room for Christelijke Gereformeerde piety and preaching. If there is unity based on Scripture and the Reformed confessions, then there must be room for a variety of accents within this unity. Kuyper cannot be called un- or neo-Reformed. There are differences in accent between Kuyper and H. Bavinck—the latter being a representative of the Secession tradition—but these differences pale in comparison to the great unity between them. With regard to the issues important to the Christelijke Gereformeerde Church, Schilder says that its appeal to the need for "experiential" (*bevindelijke*) preaching and a conscious conversion experience is a smokescreen to avoid facing God's call to Christian unity.[33] It is to make a difference of accent and homiletical approach into a confessional difference. By doing this it is the Christelijke Gereformeerde Church, and not the Reformed Churches, that has thrown up an unnecessary barrier to biblical, Reformed unity. It remains schismatic, and as an institution it cannot legitimately claim to have been blessed by God, Schilder writes in a polemical article against the daily *De Rotterdammer* in 1929. The situation is rather an "organized misunderstanding."[34] Not that Christelijke Gereformeerde members are not Christians or not Reformed! Precisely *because* Schilder sees them as Reformed Christians is he unable to accept their separate organization as legitimate.

Second, then, Schilder emphasizes God's serious call to church unity. Schilder is fundamentally arguing here that if true unity of faith exists, as it did with respect to the Christelijke Gereformeerde Church, it must lead to concrete, visible unity in church life. There is no place for separate groups of mere like-minded souls, acting apart from one another, if they are composed of genuine believers, building on the same Word and holding to the same confessions. This is not some Kuyperian attempt to organize external unity "in the flesh" at the cost of spiritual unity, as the Christelijke Gereformeerde spokesmen were claiming, but the path of obedience to the Lord of the church.

This Schilderian analysis of the situation and this call to church unity, addressed to the Christelijke Gereformeerde Church and all Reformed believers in the Netherlands, remained constants in his lifetime. They received an extra intensification after the Liberation, when concrete discussions about church unity were held between the Reformed Churches (Liberated) and the Christelijke Gereformeerde Churches (the singular name became plural in 1947). From the side of the latter it appeared that Schilder had changed. It appeared that he was now a friend, whereas previously he had been an enemy. But this is not really a proper reading of Schilder's own point of view. On the one hand, it is true that Schilder had become much more critical of Kuyper and therefore more sympathetic to the Christelijke Gereformeerde objections to Kuyper. On the other hand, he still had no intention of forming a church that would officially ban all Kuyperian ideas as intolerable. Even after the Liberation, Schilder was continually aware of the need for a church that was just as broad as the Scripture and the confessions. He maintained his objections to all synodical decisions that would bind members beyond the point at which Scripture and the confessions bound them.[35] We sense a certain tension here, since Schilder was at certain points very critical of Kuyper. But we see above all his overriding conviction regarding the need for freedom within the bounds of Scripture and the confessions.

This constancy in Schilder's attitude toward church unity is thus key to understanding his approach to the Christelijke Gereformeerde Church(es) in the period before and after the Liberation. The fact that the unity talks broke down under the same pressures as before, that is, the experiential (bevindelijke) orientation of the piety and preaching of the Christelijke Gereformeerde Churches, is explained not by Schilder's opposition to such piety and preaching, although he did thoroughly disagree with much of it, but by the refusal of the Christelijke Gereformeerde side to seek institutional unity in spite of differences in these areas. For Schilder, there *existed* unity of faith between the Reformed and the Christelijke Gereformeerde sides, in spite of clear differences, and that unity had to be brought into practice in order to be obedient to God's call.

Discontinuity: from Pro-Kuyper to Selectively Anti-Kuyper

As we have mentioned, Schilder's theological development contained certain major changes as well as certain constants. One of the most striking changes is his change of attitude to certain theological concepts of Kuyper's. While maintaining a definite affinity with Kuyper in terms of their common appeal to the infallibility of Scripture as the foundation of all theological endeavor, and to the Reformed confessions as the expression of a common theological stance, Schilder moved from being a warm defender of Kuyper on most issues in 1928 to being a sometimes severe critic of Kuyper (and particularly of Kuyper's followers) on some key issues in the 1930s and 1940s.

This development away from Kuyper was certainly not one of unadulterated antagonism. It was selective. This makes every generalization about it quite risky. In 1936 Schilder could entitle a pamphlet attacking Dutch Nazis and pacifists in the church with a famous quotation from Kuyper: "Geen Duimbreed!" ("Not Even an Inch!"— that is, no territory of the world does not belong to Jesus Christ).[36] Yet in certain key dogmatic areas regarding the "invisible and visible church," the "true and false church," and the "pluriformity of the church," Schilder departed consciously from his earlier, more Kuyperian line.

Kuyper on the Church. We may regard Abraham Kuyper's ecclesiology as containing certain basic components, within a general approach. That approach might be called Reformed orthodoxy seeking modern expression.[37] Kuyper (1837–1920) was quite strongly influenced by idealism as a student in Leiden, and this influence remained evident in his theology, even after his conversion from modernism to orthodoxy in the 1860s and early 1870s. Kuyper is enamored of the "organic," the inner connections of life uniting the world, mankind, and the church, receiving impetus for this from German romanticism (although we must be careful about assessing the degree and character of this influence).

Aspects of Kuyper's theology that impinge on his ecclesiology and that would have to be described in full include his belief in "eternal justification," the idea that the elect are essentially justified from eternity; his view of common grace, God's grace to the nonelect, by which sin is restrained and culture is made possible;[38] his belief that academic theology was a science that belonged to the realm of scientific research and thus should be carried on in a university setting, rather than in a church-controlled seminary;[39] and his belief that the state has no role in eliminating false religion, as the Belgic Confession ostensibly says in article 36, implying a rejection of "theocracy."[40]

I believe that without neglecting the above-mentioned themes and others, we can get a good sense of Kuyper's fundamental ecclesiology if we single out the following convictions as typically Kuyperian:[41]

1. The institutional church ought to be a *mother,* caring for her children in the preaching of the Word, the sacraments, and discipline. Such a mother church, which he did not find in the liberal Dutch Reformed Church of his day, Kuyper sought via reformation and union with the Secession churches in 1892.

2. The church is an *organism,* the body of Christ, the visible church knit together as one body, spread out in the world in all church formations, and indicated by baptism. For Kuyper the organic church is the source for, but is to be distinguished from, the institutional church on earth. As the organic church, all Christians may work together in the areas of politics (the Anti-Revolutionary Party), education (Christian schools and the Free University of Amsterdam), and other areas.

3. Immediate *regeneration,* working through the generations in an organic fashion, taking place in the elect as a rule in the womb or shortly after birth, is the source of power in every elect individual to live in faith, and thus of the church itself.[42] Assuming infants to be elect and thus regenerate, we baptize them, at which time the Spirit incorporates them into the church in a special way.

4. The *local church,* composed of confessing believers, is the basic unit of the church. Confederations of such churches form classes and synods, but there may be no hierarchy, each church having the same position and rights as every other church.

5. The multiformity or *pluriformity* of the church is the consequence of (1) the presence of elect individuals in all church formations, (2) the presence of autonomous true churches within more and

less pure church formations, and (3) the richness of God's truth, which cannot be confined to expression in one church formation on earth. In each country of the world various factors influence developments, so that Protestant church formations have different and sometimes conflicting forms and doctrines. Closely related to this conviction about the pluriformity of the church is the idea of the church as invisible (the elect) and visible (all professing Christians). There is in fact in every institutional church a degree of truth and a degree of falsity, and the concept that there exists one true institutional church as opposed to other false churches, a concept present in the sixteenth-century Reformation confessions (for example, the Belgic Confession), needs correction.[43] The variety of the institutional forms of the church does not hinder true unity, though the Calvinist churches have the duty to convince the others of their superior principles.

Schilder in Some Continuity with Kuyper. In two areas Schilder stayed within this Kuyperian ecclesiological frame: first, with respect to seeing the institutional church as a mother, a pure Reformed church raising her sons and daughters for service to the Father; and second, with respect to seeing the church as being composed of autonomous local churches, federated together to form a church federation (*kerkverband*), although remaining true churches even without such a relation. This latter conviction was the key concept of the Doleantie view of church order, elaborately defended by Kuyper and his colleague at the Free University F. L. Rutgers (1836–1917).[44] During the 1880s, fierce debates had raged between Secession spokesmen, defending the singular name of their church (Christelijke Gereformeerde *Kerk*), the national character of their church formation, and the power of classes and synods regarding local churches, and the Doleantie spokesmen, defending the theory of the autonomy of local congregations. At the time of the union in 1892, the Doleantie theory had proved convincing and victorious, resulting in a plural name for the new church (Gereformeerde *Kerken* [Reformed Churches]) and a church polity emphasizing the lack of hierarchy and the full rights of local churches.

In these areas, seeing the need for a truly Reformed institutional church, and conceiving of the institutional church as fundamentally the local church, Schilder shows strong continuity with Kuyper, and it is in fact in the area of church polity and order that Schilder remains the most Kuyperian. At the time of the Liberation, Schilder's chief accusation in the direction of the general synod was that it had abandoned the principles of Reformed (Doleantie) church polity and established a hierarchy over the local churches.

Nevertheless, it is in his deviations from Kuyper that Schilder caused the most commotion in the 1930s, and it is to these deviations that we now turn our attention.

Schilder Moving Away from Kuyper. Whereas Schilder in the 1920s could agree with Kuyper on the organic and invisible church, and so support general cooperation between Christians across church boundaries in politics, education, journalism, and new media (Schilder was one of the founders of the interchurch radio organization named the NCRV in the 1920s),[45] after the establishment of the Hersteld Verband (restored federation) churches under the leadership of Geelkerken in 1926, Schilder became more critical about how "pluriformity" was being put into practice. He could not accept the idea that followers of Geelkerken or Barthians could be professors at the Free University of Amsterdam or could have access to the NCRV. He could even speak about the "yoke" of interchurch activities in 1930.[46]

This dissatisfaction with the practice of certain interchurch activities broadened in the 1930s to a questioning of the concept of church pluriformity itself. When Kuyperians and others in the Reformed Churches attempted to defend various interchurch activities, such as an international organization of Calvinists that would allow Hersteld Verband spokesmen and Barthians to participate, using the theory of the pluriformity of the church to defend this policy, Schilder reacted by critically reassessing the theory itself.[47]

As we noted in discussing Schilder's own theological continuity, he had always refused to accept the legitimacy of the existence of the Christelijke Gereformeerde Church (along with Kuyperians such as the law professor D. P. D. Fabius). Now, in the polemics of the 1930s, this attitude deepened to shape his own theorizing about the church and its nature. To speak of true and false churches was not a judgment about persons, but about the norms of God's gathering, revealed in the Word.[48] As Schilder continued his polemics, he found

himself more and more in agreement with the old Secession opponents of Kuyper, before the union of 1892, such as H. Beuker and
F. M. Ten Hoor, who had criticized Kuyper for being too soft on the
Dutch Reformed Church.[49] Whereas in the tradition of the Secession
it had been commonplace to label the Dutch Reformed Church a false
church, Kuyper and the Doleantie leaders had refused to speak in
such black-and-white terms. They could speak of a false hierarchy,
trying to run the whole church, but since local churches were the only
real forms of the church, and since regeneration formed the invisible
church, they could not bring themselves to call the Dutch Reformed
Church as a whole a false church. This is in contrast to the views of
Beuker and Ten Hoor, for whom it was imperative to indict the Dutch
Reformed Church as a false church, considering how the Belgic Confession calls believers to separate from those who do not belong to
the church (article 28) and in light of the clear teaching about the true
church and the false church that it gives in article 29.

In finding old Secession allies against Kuyper in this area,
Schilder found confessional support in the text of the Belgic Confession, which says in article 29 that "these two churches [the true and
the false] are easily recognized and distinguished from one another."

Instead of the old organic church ideas, linked to the pluensity-
mity of the church and the concepts of an invisible and a visible
church, Schilder developed an alternative, combining confessional
faithfulness with his new "dynamic" view of the church. We will
look shortly in more depth at this latter concept, a new development
in the Reformed tradition.

After the Liberation Schilder and his colleagues charted a new
course for Christian politics, education, and journalism. These areas
came to be seen by Schilder more and more as demanding the same
criteria as in the church. That is, church membership became more
and more the criterion for cooperation. Kuyper's ideas about the organic, pluralistic church were rejected in favor of reformation—in
the church and, flowing from this, in all of life. Although Schilder
was tentative about the concrete outworkings of the broadening of
the radius of this reformation to politics, in the areas of journalism
and education it was soon a chief emphasis. For example, the forming of (Liberated) Reformed schools became a hallmark of Liberated

thinking. Although Schilder died in 1952, before this process of "continuing reformation" was completed, we may say that it was a logical consequence of his ecclesiology.

We see then how in Schilder's own theological development, he distanced himself from certain Kuyperian ecclesiastical views and so in key ways became an anti-Kuyperian.

DISCONTINUITY: A CHANGE IN THE THEOLOGY OF THE COVENANT

Another area of eventual difference from Kuyper was regeneration. Whereas Kuyper laid the emphasis on (immediate) regeneration by the Holy Spirit as the motor and soul of the church, Schilder, without denying the importance of regeneration, emphasized its mediation through the Word and the fact that the *covenant* is not defined by regeneration.

Many have called attention to the centrality of the covenant in Schilder's theology of the church.[50] It is in this connection important to realize, however, that Schilder's view of the covenant underwent a distinct change. And it is only his later theology of the covenant that he uses to bolster his anti-Kuyperian ecclesiastical ideas.

As we have seen, in the 1920s Schilder was a convinced follower of "Dort, Kuyper, and Bavinck." This was also true with regard to the theology of the covenant. In the view of Kuyper and Bavinck, who saw the covenant in light of eternal election, God makes His covenant of grace so that it has two sides: an outward side and an inward side, or in other words, an external form and inward substance. Outwardly, all believers and their children are in the covenant. Inwardly, only the elect are genuinely members of the covenant.

In 1934 Schilder began to change his view. Fearing the misuse of an invisible church theory construed in terms of all the elect, Schilder received stimulus from various sources to see the covenant in a different way. In a polemical address criticizing the Dutch Reformed Church in 1935, Schilder lays emphasis on "covenant faithfulness" as constituent to the "church as mother."[51] Over against the "quietism" in the Dutch Reformed Church, Schilder says that covenant faithfulness leads to institutional *church* faithfulness.[52] This is no passive thing, but part of our responsibility as believers.

We see Schilder eventually parting with the Kuyperian-Bavinck-ian theology of the covenant, which connected the covenant directly with eternal election. For Schilder in his mature thinking, God makes His covenant with believers and their children. There are not two sides of this covenant, in the sense of a substance and a form, but rather two *reactions* to the single covenant of grace, one of obedience and another of disobedience. Children of believers are not merely to be regarded as in the (inner, substantial) covenant, but they are genuinely and really in the (nondualistic) covenant.

This change of his view of the covenant was also one that Schilder carried through with help from aspects of the Secession tradition. For example, Helenius de Cock and Ten Hoor had held a similar view, over against the Kuyperian tendency to identify the covenant with election. This was not entirely a unanimous Secession point of view, however, since the experiential (bevindelijke) concept of covenant, present in the Secession tradition, also portrayed the covenant as having two sides, or substance and form, with the substantial covenant of grace being made only with the elect.

In Schilder's covenantal views we see a distinct shift, but one that supported his shift away from Kuyperian ecclesiology in the direction of what he conceived to be a more confessional and more biblical position.

Continuity and Discontinuity: Schilder and the Reformed Tradition

If we may speak of a distinct Reformed ecclesiology, then we are probably correct to see Calvin as the most important of the chief sources for such an ecclesiology, distinct from Roman Catholic, Lutheran, and Anabaptist concepts. At the time of and after Calvin, Reformed ecclesiology developed in various directions, leaving its marks in various confessional documents, works of dogmatics, and polemical debates, but key features remained the same.

In the Reformed tradition we see at least two constants: the authority of the Word and the derivative authority of the Reformed confessions in the church. But although a great degree of harmony is evident in the Reformed creeds of the sixteenth century,[53] also typical of these creeds is a startling diversity with respect to church form and polity. The Swiss, the French, the Hungarian, the Dutch, and the English and Scottish churches and other national and provincial churches developed in different ecclesiastical ways. The Episcopal Anglican Church generally regarded itself, until the Arminian reaction after the Synod of Dort, as a Reformed, Bullingerian and Calvinistic church. And the divines of Westminster saw themselves as building on this heritage. All the same, they brought a reformation to the form of the Church of England, replacing Episcopalianism with Presbyterianism. And at the same time in England and in the American colonies we see Calvinistic Congregationalism stressing the autonomy of local congregations, over against bishops but also over against the presbyteries of the Westminster church order.

In spite of this variety of church polity in the Calvinistic tradition, ranging from Episcopalianism (Ussher) to Congregationalism (John Owen), we see much common language in the confessions and dogmatics of the Reformed theologians of the sixteenth to eighteenth centuries. That Heinrich Heppe could compile a "Reformed dogmatics" of this period from publications dating from 1559 (Calvin's *Institutes*) to Endeman (1777–78), with a synthesized chapter titled "The Church,"[54] indicates the degree of unity that existed. This can be maintained without ignoring important differences, differences to which we shall call attention.

Historically, the fact that representatives from the Anglican Church and various continental Reformed churches could be present at the Synod of Dort in 1618 and reach substantial unity on the issues raised by the Arminians indicates a unity of faith *as churches* that could transcend, at least temporarily, the issue of church polity. The Canons of Dort are in a genuine sense a product of international, Reformed, *ecclesiastical* ecumenism.

CONTINUITY: REFORMED DOCTRINE AND LIFE IN THE CHURCH

The Reformed reformation in Europe in the sixteenth century, which continued in the centuries that followed, can be characterized as holding to the three *solas* of the Lutheran reformation (*Sola Scriptura,*

Sola Gratia, Sola Fide). Further, in all Reformed churches the old orthodox confessions of the early church regarding the Trinity and the person of Christ (Nicea, Chalcedon) were continued.

In the Reformed tradition it is the church, not the state, and not merely individual believers, that must maintain these doctrinal distinctives, this confessional stance. Much more than in the Lutheran tradition, there is here an emphasis on internal church discipline as a hallmark of vital church life. The marks of the church in the Reformed confessions maintain the Lutheran emphasis on the Word and the sacraments, combined with either implicit or explicit demands for church discipline as a constitutive mark of the church of Christ.

Clearly, Klaas Schilder's convictions carry on this Reformed tradition in practically all areas of his faith-convictions and theology, including, most definitely, ecclesiology. For him, as we have seen, the authority of God's Word is a sine qua non not only for personal salvation, but for authentic, true church life. In his writings he continues to reject humanism and Roman Catholic synergism, in line with the Reformation emphasis on the sovereignty of God's grace and the total depravity of man. In his magnum opus, the unfinished, monumental, four-volume treatise on the Heidelberg Catechism, he continues the criticism of the Roman Catholic and Arminian defense of man's free will, typical of Reformed polemics since Calvin and the Synod of Dort. On all major points of intraconfessional controversy, Schilder stands clearly and consciously on the side of the Reformed fathers.

This continuity between the mainstream of the Reformed tradition and Schilder is incontestable. It is therefore strange to hear him being accused of an un-Reformed "churchism" when his ecclesiology is being discussed.[55] How is such an accusation possible, and could it be valid?

Selectivity in Continuity: Reaching Back. The key to answering this question is to see *how* Schilder connects with his Reformed past. This connection is a selective one, with Schilder in general reaching back to Calvin and the early Reformation for support and for linkage with new concepts as he rethinks past Reformed views. J. Kamphuis typified Schilder's theology as a theology in a "sympathetic-critical" relation to past Reformed orthodoxy.[56] This could give the impression that Schilder was critical of all the explicit *positions* in the gamut of Reformed theology from Calvin to the eighteenth century, while being sympathetic to its *aims*. However, this would be a false impression. Schilder, in his selective agreement with past Reformed *positions* (not merely intentions), almost uniformly follows a pattern of distinguishing between later scholastic orthodoxy and early Reformed *confessions* and related theology—especially Calvin, finding or at least claiming agreement with the latter, and questioning the formulations of the later scholastics.[57] This is not always Schilder's method, but it is the tendency of his mind.

The suggestion of homogeneous continuity between Calvin and later Reformed orthodoxy produced by Heppe's *Reformed Dogmatics* needs to be taken with a necessary dose of critical appraisal. There are certain important discontinuities, as well as many continuities, in the early Reformed tradition. This is admitted by all researchers, and often exaggerated for polemical purposes (the supposed contrast between Calvin and his successor Beza with respect to the doctrine of atonement is a common example),[58] but for assessing Schilder's relation to Reformed orthodoxy it is especially important.

The Covenant. We may take the doctrine of the covenant, central in Schilder's later ecclesiology, as a case in point. After the Synod of Dort, and perhaps as early as Olevianus, Reformed theology tended to think of God's covenant as being made "substantially" with the elect. Kuyper and Bavinck had thus some legitimate historical grounds for calling their doctrine of the covenant, in which it is made substantially with the elect, *the* Reformed position. However, as Schilder develops his revised view of the covenant, he reaches back to Calvin for support in seeing the covenant as a *single* covenant of grace made with believers and all their children, as distinguished from eternal election by which only some, and not all, of such children will be saved.[59] Schilder appeals then to a continuity with Calvin,[60] which is at the same time a discontinuity between Calvin and the later Reformed tradition, in order to build his own Reformed doctrine of the covenant.

The Belgic Confession. It cannot be denied that Schilder attempts to take articles 27–29 of the Belgic Confession much more seriously than various interpreters of the Kuyper and Bavinck tradition had done. Kuyper had maintained that article 29, speaking in terms of two easily identifiable entities, the true church and the false church, was no longer directly viable in the modern world. K. Dijk had tried to defend a church pluriformity in combination with an adherence to these articles in 1920.[61] But it was certainly Schilder who was the closest to the plain language of these articles in his polemics of the 1930s.

It was nothing new to reintroduce in a modern way the position of many Secession spokesmen before the union of 1892, and of such Secession spokesmen in the united churches—as G. Doekes had done when he defended the "strict" interpretation of the Belgic Confession articles about the church in 1909.[62]

What is of interest to us at this moment is to see Schilder reaching back to the language of the Belgic Confession in his ecclesiastical polemics, indicating his firm connection to and continuity with the Reformed tradition of the sixteenth century. In reaching back in agreement, Schilder is simultaneously calling various later orthodox concepts and formulations into question. And sometimes, he merely rejects the scholastic positions without seeking any particular help from Calvin, early confessions, or any other theological source. Here we see Schilder thinking in conscious discontinuity with the past and yet always seeking to remain Reformed, reasoning from the text of Scripture.

DISCONTINUITY: OLD CONCEPTS REPLACED BY NEW

Schilder's continuity with the Reformed tradition is clear. But he was not satisfied with mere continuity, even continuity with Calvin. And he was not satisfied with a mere repetition of the language of the confession. For as a pastor and a theologian, he was called to search the Scriptures, and in light of that search to attempt to correct past theological formulas and construct new theological patterns of truth to serve genuine reformation. This meant on occasion choosing for discontinuity with a long tradition of terminology and conceptualization.

The Church Militant on Earth and Triumphant in Heaven? A clear example of Schilder's method of conscious choosing for discontinuity is his rejection of the later scholastic Reformed view of the church being militant on earth and triumphant in heaven. Heppe summarizes this position as Reformed theologians framed it.

> The Church embraces both the believers blessedly at rest and those alive on earth. So *ratione status ecclesiae* (from the nature of the Church's status) there belongs essentially to the concept of the Church the distinction between the *ecclesia triumphans* and the *ecclesia militans*. The former is the community of those who have fallen asleep in true faith here on earth and have now entered upon the condition of perfect freedom from sin and death, upon God's perfect peace and upon perfect blessedness. The latter, of which we have to speak particularly here, is the community of believers here on earth.[63]

But Schilder, appealing to Scripture, sees the church on earth triumphing by faith daily, while the church in heaven, praying for the coming judgment, is not yet wholly at rest, but still struggling (Rev. 5 and 11). The eschatological tension of the church in our moment in time—before the Second Coming—can be lost, Schilder claims, if this is not kept in consideration.

Schilder does not totally reject the old distinction out of hand,[64] but he says that one can just as legitimately speak of the triumphant church on earth and the militant church in heaven. In other words, these scholastic distinctions are *not sufficient* and can be *misleading*. If one uses these distinctions as absolutes, one soon runs into problems with Scripture interpretation and with practical application. Schilder considers the traditional Reformed distinction between the church militant and the church triumphant a residue of medieval scholastic and prescholastic theology. In a Platonic way, the church in heaven was made the more important church, in a hierarchy of being, and the church on earth was relativized.[65] But saints composing the church in heaven are not wholly perfect or perfected, waiting as they are for the bodily resurrection. The church is still *being gathered,* and is nowhere at rest or perfect, before the Second Coming.[66]

In this way Schilder makes a break with the terminology for the church found in much Reformed orthodoxy, due to its insufficient biblical base and its being influenced by non-Christian philosophy.

This emphasis on God's dynamic, ongoing work of gathering the church, as well as on biblical history and eschatology as the proper setting for a more adequate doctrine of the church, was expressed by Schilder in nineteen theses about the church, which he published in *De Reformatie* in 1935.[67] They show his positive attempt to think anew about the church in the Reformed tradition. In them we hear his rejection of the old militant/triumphant church terminology, as well as his typically Schilderian dogmatic wrestling to see the church in a more biblical way.

The Movement of the Gathering of the Church: A Selection from the Nineteen Theses of 1935. We may call these propositions some of the most vivid evidence of Schilder's striving toward doctrinal and ecclesiastical reform and renewal, under the authority of Scripture and in harmony with the Reformed confessions—but signalling a break with certain old distinctions and inadequate formulations. As a kind of summary of Schilder's theology of the church, they give us documentation of his passion and sophistication in theology, his interactions with past dogmatic formulations, and his attempt to be true to Scripture. In what follows I give my own translation of a selection from these theses, with some commentary.

1. That a church exists—this one cannot see, but only *believe.* Every definition of the essence of the church (supposing that it is possible to speak about such an "essence") using that which one can see in the world here below, or on the grounds of other axioms than the Scripture has *revealed,* is thus a work of nonbelief or unbelief—even if many truths may be expressed.[68] "Discovering" or "inventing" truths is pride in this case as well.

Comment: Here Schilder is in clear continuity with the entire Reformed tradition.[69] Although that tradition quickly goes on to speak of an "invisible church,"[70] which Schilder does not want to do, he expresses by this proposition solidarity with the Reformed tradition in opposing a Roman Catholic absolutizing of the church institute, as well as rejecting the empirical approach of modern theology to the church. What we believe about the church must be determined by Scripture and nothing else.

> 2. "The" church has never been observed. No one has ever seen "the" church. No one has ever seen "humanity." No one has ever seen the Dutch people or any other people. For the church is never "finished," just as little as humanity or a people are "finished." Only when the last elect person will have come to faith and will be carrying on a life of faith will "the" church have reached her *pleroma* [fullness]. Even then, however, the "seeing" of it, in one and the same way of "seeing," will be possible only on the other side of the boundary that divides this age from the coming one.

Comment: Here again Schilder is guarding himself against naively positing a simplistic visible church to replace the old invisible/visible church theory. His orientation to the future is evident.

> 3. Strictly speaking, there is thus not yet a "visible" church. There are just temporary and local *parts* and *activities* of such parts of the church to be seen. For example: certain ways of structuring and organization of the life of such parts of the church in a certain period of time (the Old Testament, the New Testament, before and after a reformation) or in a certain place (on earth; in heaven; in the Netherlands, Russia, or Java; and so on).

Comment: Schilder is very careful in the way in which he is structuring his alternative to the Kuyperian ecclesiology. He does this by paying attention to the time-bound character of our ability to see the church, and to the eschatological orientation of the church's existence ("not *yet* a 'visible' church"). That "the church" is not visible, and that we derive all that we know of the church's essence from

Scripture, does not prevent us from talking meaningfully about parts and activities of the church on earth in our time, which we can indeed observe.

> 4. Inasmuch as the concept of "invisible" is determined by the concept of "visible," the need to speak about an "invisible church" is eliminated.

Comment: Schilder phrases his criticism of scholastic Reformed and Kuyperian orthodoxy in such a way as to disarm his critics. Instead of totally rejecting the invisible church, he denies the existence of the visible church, and thereby the need to create an artificial theory of the invisible church.

> 5. The church is willed by God; the Son of God indubitably gathers for Himself a congregation, chosen to eternal life, by his Spirit and Word. He does this from the beginning of the world to its end. He is thus busy with this activity today, and tomorrow, and until the final day. He is thus at work, with this objective, in the *"imperfect present"* tense. Suppose that there is only one carpenter in the whole world, who needs all of history to make one table, which he will deliver at the end. Surely no one can commend the quality of the man's work, so long as the praise is based on some "phenomenologically" developed argument about the "visible" table and the "invisible" table that the carpenter is making. So, in the same way, no one should tire the Son of God with doxologies based on "phenomenologically" developed theories about "the" "visible" church and "the" "invisible" church. How do we know what the carpenter's table will look like, supposing that there is only one carpenter in the world and only one table . . . and supposing that we ourselves are the wood that he cuts and carves in order to make his table? "The" church has never ever been a phenomenon; further, there is only *one* Lord, and only *one* church is being made, *once*. Socrates cannot form a "concept" of the church here, for there is only *one* church; and to form concepts, he needs more than one "specimen."

And Plato can't do it either; already the simple fact that the church is divided over two "worlds," ever since the first Expiration of breath from human nostrils (the first death), . . . prevents Plato, with his teaching about the two worlds, from constructing an "essence" of the church. And furthermore, since no one can say something about the church *without the Scripture,* every word about the church is *bound to Scripture.*

Comment: This is the first proposition that mentions God's gathering of the church, Schilder's alternative to the invisible/visible church theory, building on the language of the Heidelberg Catechism, Lord's Day 21.[71] He continues this rejection of "empirically" based church theories by rejecting also the philosophical concept of a church constructed with the help of the Platonic distinction between the higher world of the ideas and the lower world of the phenomena.

6. As has already been said, the church is gathered (brought together) every day by the living Lord (*Kurios*) Jesus Christ. This activity of gathering occurs daily in the "imperfect present" tense. Every distinction between the "being" and the "well-being," between the "invisible" church and the "visible" church, between the church as "organism" and the church as "institute," is therefore false and fatal, if it disengages (abstracts) the *coming together* of believers, occurring daily in the imperfect present tense, from the *bringing together* of believers by Jesus Christ (the congregation of believers), which likewise takes place daily in the "imperfect present" tense.

Comment: Schilder here presents his alternative to Kuyperian ecclesiology, at the same time rejecting scholastic Reformed dualities. They are inadequate because they do not take into account Christ's actual ongoing work of gathering the church. If they would do this, and thus would not abstract the human responsibility to come together from the divine activity of bringing together, Schilder implies that such dualities might still be able to be used.

7. Christ's *work of bringing together* is the daily focus of His prayer. It is thus the way toward the completion of the world. Consequently, one can be His coworker, and thus really social, only if one accomplishes the work of gathering the church, insofar as faith can see it, in obedience to His commandments. His revealed Word alone indicates to us the paths along which His prayer proceeds [*beweegt*] and seeks to move [*beweegt*] the Father, and does indeed move Him into moving us [*tot het bewegen-van-ons*].

Comment: A typical Schilderian playing with words and concepts! And the meaning is key to Schilder's ecclesiology. Believers are Christ's coworkers in a real sense, if they gather with Him in obedience. Divine power engages human energy in the one work of church gathering. Scripture reveals how Christ prays (for example, in John 17), and this is the source of the dynamism for the reality of the church.

8. Making election, or faith, or the demonstrable sanctification of the individual (as if this had to be "cultivated," "tended," or "strengthened") the principle of bringing together believers and holding them together, without asking whether there is an actual "coworking" with Christ, who is gathering the church together, can therefore be considered a disobedient way to determine the formation of the church. Just as the formation of the family may not be made dependent upon the question of how a particular family can find rest in an inwardly directed self-satisfaction, but must rather take place with the desire that God would bring forth the body of His children through us, so too every church reformation, instead of asking how a particular fellowship of believers may find rest in their *given* state of being together, must continually be determined by the question "How is Christ gathering the body of His elect out of and through us?"

Comment: Again we see Schilder reorienting the doctrine of the church to the activity of Christ and the activity of believers in cooperation with Him. The emphasis is not on individual salvation but on obedience and corporate responsibility in the actual formation of actual local churches.

9. Hence the view of the church as "Heilsanstalt" (institution for salvation) is absolutely condemned.

10. Hereby it has also been acknowledged that the will to gather and the deed of gathering the believers into *one* body form a constitutive "mark" of the church of the first order. "The will to ecumenism" [*oecumenisch-willen*] is the primary mark of the church; the question as to *how* and *when* a church formation is truly ecumenical can be answered only by the declared, revealed, expressed will of God.

Comment: Schilder shows how his alternative to Kuyperian ecclesiology is not pietistic, quietistic, or passive. He is even willing to take the daring step of creating a "primary mark" of the true church above the marks in the Belgic Confession, article 29, to do this. Reformed ecumenism, living out of the will of God, is a living reality.

11. Since the "will to gather believers" from all places in every moment of history is the first mark of the church (because in this Christ's work is carried out in our working together with Him), it is a basic mistake of the first order to attempt to establish "marks" of the church or "divisions" of the church, if these criteria either contradict or are abstracted from this first mark.

Comment: Here, in a manner similar to that in which he connects the scholastic terminology to the gathering of Christ, Schilder connects the traditional marks and divisions to this dynamic priority of the will to ecumenism.

12. A mistake of this sort is made when, for example, marks of the *church* (a *society* of people) are defined in the categories of *strictly personal* events or experiences. For *personal* experiences are not real criteria for a gathering, the formation of a community, *as such*.

Comment: A reiteration of Schilder's rejection of personal soteriological categories as central to the church.

> 13. This objectionable method is followed, for example, in many cases when distinctions are made between the "invisible" church and the "visible" church, or between the "militant" church and the "triumphant" church. In the case of the first distinction, it is indubitably so that often people think of the question of whether someone has faith or not; and in the case of the second distinction, the question often arises as to whether someone has still to fight against the sins and disasters of this dispensation or not. But both questions are addressing strictly *personal* matters of biography.

Comment: Here Schilder is more directly attacking the views of the "experiential" groups that reject church union on the grounds of the priority of individual conversion.

> 14. Naturally, such strictly personal matters have significance in the further development or degeneration of the life of the church. But this is certainly no reason to make such distinctions special principles of division or principles of recognition specifically with respect to the CHURCH. It is easy to see that such distinctions are similarly applicable to the life and fortunes of nonchurch organizations. *Every* Christian organization suffers if there are hypocrites in it. Every organization of believing people, including *nonecclesiastical [niet-kerkelijk]* ones, is "invisible," insofar as one cannot "see" faith (any more than one can "see" the power of thought or melancholy, for example), and "visible," insofar as faith cannot *avoid* expressing itself openly (any more than the power of thought or melancholy can avoid expressing itself openly). . . .

Comment: Schilder is pointing out the need for specifically ecclesiastical categories in talking about the church.

15. Such criteria, which do not take into consideration the (church) *gathering* factor, are the cause of much misunderstanding with regard to the church.

16. So, the distinction between "visible" church and the "invisible" church, which was developed in *this* way, has often had the consequence that whole societies of sectarian origin and practice were nevertheless regarded as "true churches," for the simple reason that that which is invisible (faith) was expected from their members. But of course this also is the case with every "conventicle" of pious believers . . . and with every Christian sport club! However, the question about what one did to GATHER with Christ was no longer seen to be an issue of primary importance for one's conscience. The primary stipulation of the law of the CHURCH was neglected.

17. Indeed, a church-in-heaven that sins in a similar way was even invented: the so-called triumphant church above, as opposed to the militant one here below. The triumph of the (only initially) blessed ones was then distinguished from the "struggle" in which the same persons, now blessed, had been engaged on earth. On the basis of this strictly *personal* experience, a scheme of *church*-classification was then given. But precisely because the church is still church in the making (divided over two places, "above" and "below") it can never say that in its work of gathering it already has arrived at the stage of communal triumph. Triumphing (in the present-*perfect* tense) is done only by one who is finished. Christ as Gatherer of the church is as yet not finished by far. Hence also the church in its church-affairs is not yet ready or completed by far. Christ is indeed triumphing daily in the present-*progressive* tense; but this also applies (through Him) to the so-called militant church (more than conquerers; faith conquers the world). Christ is triumphing in the present-progressive tense. (His struggle is a "prospering" struggle). But the same thing applies also to the so-called triumphant church. It struggles daily in its prayers (by far the keenest weapon, according to Revelation 6 and 11). So it, too, seeks to have the

church reach completion. A "triumphant church" that would abstract (separate) its triumph from the one concrete church struggle (divided over both divisions, above and below) would be sectarian, just like the "society for mutual upbuilding," the schismatic church, and the conventicle (see 16).

18. In the light of these thoughts one discerns the abhorrent nature of sectarianism. It runs counter to the prayers of Christ and of the (initially) blessed ones. It turns the weapon of the division of the believers that are below against the weapon of the (also still) believing ones that are above. It is therefore the "abomination of desolation" in the very place where it least belongs.

19. The so-called militant church therefore triumphs daily; the so-called triumphant church is daily engaged in struggle. In all its locations (on earth and in heaven) the church struggles and triumphs from moment to moment and proves thereby that it sees its cooperation with the gathering Christ as the distinguishing mark of its life.

Conclusion: Schilder Is Not Sectarian

In these theses we see the theologian Schilder at work, interacting with and criticizing the past, seeking new paths for a Reformed ecclesiology. If we may now attempt to answer the question that we posed at the beginning of this article, it has become quite clear, I believe, that Schilder's ecclesiology was neither absolutizing with regard to the visible church nor sectarian. He was a Reformed theologian who stood firmly in the orthodox Reformed tradition, but who, from within that tradition, sought to listen to Scripture and seek alternatives for the less-than-biblical ecclesiologies, past and present, that he saw around him. He was a polemical theologian, to be sure, but one who never forgot to make true biblical ecumenism his constant and highest goal.

In our day of liberal ecclesiastical ecumenism, without agreement about the authority of Scripture, and evangelical cooperation without church unity, it would be good to listen to the voice of Klaas

Schilder. He sought concrete church unity, but only on the firm basis of God's Word. He sought to avoid the dilemma of a liberal church union without the Word or an orthodox Protestant movement with the Bible as its basis but without church unity. In this sense, he remains prophetic and challenging to both groups in our day.

Notes

1. Cf. R. H. Bremmer, "Schilder, Klaas," in D. Nauta et al., *Biografisch Lexicon voor de Geschiedenis van het Nederlandse Protestantisme* (Biographical Lexicon of the History of Protestantism in the Netherlands) (Kampen: Kok, 1978), 1:317.

2. Schilder's theological opponent H. H. Kuyper, a professor at the Free University of Amsterdam, obviously contrasts Calvin with Schilder in H. H. Kuyper, *De Katholiciteit der Gereformeerde Kerken. Afscheidscollege, 1 juni, 1937* (The Catholicity of the Reformed Churches. Farewell lecture, June 1, 1937) (Kampen: Kok, 1937), 6: "Thus, Calvin was averse to all sectarianism, which shuts itself up within the narrow walls of its own Church and does not recognize nor desires to have fellowship with any other Church."

3. In the present article the name Reformed Churches is used for the Gereformeerde Kerken in Nederland (GKN); this name was chosen by the churches of the Secession (1834) and those of the *Doleantie* (1886) when they united in 1892. Both groups had separated from the Dutch Reformed State Church because of its liberalism. This latter church, the Hervormde Kerk, is referred to as the Dutch Reformed Church. The churches that liberated themselves in 1944 from unwarranted doctrinal pronouncements and church-political actions of the synods of the Reformed Churches are here called Reformed Churches (Liberated). Another group of Reformed churches, which came from the Secession but did not join the Union of 1892, is called the Christelijke Gereformeerde Churches (churches closely related to the Free Reformed Churches in North America); this name is left untranslated to avoid confusion with the Christian Reformed Church in North America.

4. H. D. J. Smit, "Gehoorzamen: Achter Christus Aan! Schilder Over de Kerk," (Obeying: Following Christ! Schilder on the Church) in J. Douma et al., eds., *K. Schilder: Aspecten Van Zijn Werk* (Barneveld: De Vuurbaak, 1990), 66–71.

5. Smit, "Gehoorzamen," 83–85.

6. Another Liberated theologian who has commented recently on Schilder's ecclesiology is C. Trimp in his article "De kerk bij A. Kuyper en K. Schilder" (The Church According to A. Kuyper and K. Schilder), which appears in W. van't Spijker et al., *De Kerk: Wezen, Weg en Werk van de Kerk Naar Reformatorische Opvatting* (The Church: Its Essence, Way and Work According to the Reformed View) (Kampen: De Groot Goudriaan, 1990), 191–201. Trimp singles out the following aspects of Schilder's ecclesiology for attention: the church

as the work of Christ (pp. 194–95); the dynamic of the marks of the church (p. 195); the church and human responsibility (pp. 195–96); and a threefold appeal—to the Reformed Churches, to the Dutch Reformed Church, and to the Christelijke Gereformeerde Churches (pp. 196–201). Earlier, G. C. Berkouwer had discussed Schilder's ecclesiology in *De Kerk* (The Church), vol. 1. of Dogmatische Studiën (Kampen: Kok, 1970), 19–21. See the one-volume, shortened English edition of the two-volume Dutch work, G. C. Berkouwer, *The Church,* Studies in Dogmatics (Grand Rapids: Eerdmans, 1976), 19–23. Berkouwer has commented again more recently on Schilder's ecclesiology in *Zoeken en Vinden: Herinneringen en Ervaringen* (Seeking and Finding: Memories and Experiences) (Kampen: Kok, 1989), 246–54.

7. See J. de Bruijn and G. Harinck, eds., *Geen Duimbreed! Facetten van Leven en Werk van Prof. Dr. K. Schilder, 1890–1952* (Baarn: Ten Have, 1990); G. Puchinger, ed., *Ontmoetingen met Schilder* (Encounters with Schilder) (Kampen: Kok, 1990). For other works treating Schilder's theology, see J. J. C. Dee, *K. Schilder, Zijn Leven en Werk* (K. Schilder, His Life and Work) (Goes: Oosterbaan & Le Cointre, 1990), 1:11–14.

8. For an overview of Schilder's theological development, see Bremmer, "Schilder, Klaas," 315–18.

9. On A. G. Honig and his *Handboek van de Gereformeerde Dogmatiek* (Handbook of Reformed Dogmatics) (Kampen: Kok, 1938), see J. Kamphuis, "Afscheid van 'Honig'" (Goodbye to Honig), *De Reformatie* 57, no. 3 (1981), 33–36; no. 4 (1981), 49–53; no. 5 (1981), 65–68.

10. Dee, *K. Schilder,* 163.

11. Smit, "Gehoorzamen," 75.

12. See K. Schilder, *Verzamelde Werken: De Kerk* (Collected Works: The Church) (Goes: Oosterbaan & Le Cointre, 1960–65), 1:120–21.

13. K. Schilder, *De Kerk. College-dictaat* (The Church. Lecture Notes), ed. J. Kamphuis (Kampen: van den Berg, 1978), 42. This material is taken from lectures and was published without Schilder's authority. It does, however, let us hear Schilder's actual voice as a professor.

14. See S. A. Strauss, *Alles of Niks. K. Schilder Oor die Verbond* (All or Nothing. K. Schilder on the Covenant), diss. (Pretoria: Patmos, 1982), 23–25. Strauss, quoting J. Kamphuis, sees Schilder as remaining a fundamentally loyal pupil of Kuyper's, even in criticism, because he dealt with what his "teacher" had brought up: common grace, the pluriformity of the church, and covenant and baptism (p. 25). "Loyal pupil" suggests a lasting congeniality. I question the depth of this congeniality, especially in the light of Schilder's criticism of Kuyper after the Liberation of 1944.

15. K. Schilder, "Tegenstrijdigheden in den Bijbel" (Contradictions in the Bible), in C. Veenhof, ed., *Om Woord en Kerk* (For the Sake of Word and Church) (Goes: Oosterbaan & Le Cointre, 1948–53), 3:65.

16. Schilder, "Tegenstrijdigheden in den Bijbel," 66.

17. Ibid., 94.

18. Cf. Schilder's criticism of Van Niftrik in K. Schilder, "Om den Bijbel" (Concerning the Bible), in Schilder, *Verzamelde Werken: De Kerk,* 3:166.

19. Cf. G. Harinck, "Vernieuwing en Verwarring. Klaas Schilder en het Gereformeerde Studentenleven in Verband met de Kwestie-Geelkerken" (Renewal and Confusion. Klaas Schilder and Reformed Student Life in the Matter of the Geelkerken Case), in D. T. Kuiper, ed., *Jaarboek voor de Geschiedenis van de Gereformeerde Kerken in Nederland* (Yearbook for the History of the Reformed Churches in the Netherlands) (Kampen: Kok, 1989), 3:136–57.

20. Schilder, "Om den Bijbel," 164–68.

21. K. Schilder, "Het Smoesje inzake de Schijnheilige Smoesjes" (The Fib Concerning the Hypocritical Fibs), in *Verzamelde Werken: De Kerk,* 3:168.

22. The English text of the Belgic Confession may be found in *Book of Praise,* rev. ed. (Winnipeg: Premier, 1987), 444. For the original text see J. N. Bakhuizen van den Brink, ed., *De Nederlandse Belijdenisgeschriften* (Amsterdam: Ton Bolland, 1976), 78.

23. Schilder says that he is waiting for the Dutch Reformed Church to demonstrate its avowed reformation by "a clear confession, which, for example, is true to Scripture and its content, and which excludes modernism and Barthianism from the Church" (Schilder, "Het Smoesje," 168).

24. K. Schilder, "Barth Over Pluriformiteit," in Schilder, *Verzamelde Werken: De Kerk,* 3:231.

25. Cf. J. de Jong, *Accommodatio Dei: A Theme in K. Schilder's Theology of Revelation* (Kampen: Mondiss, 1990), 12: "He urged all to a sympathetic-critical assessment of their tradition, testing both the ecclesiastical and theological heritage by the light of the only abiding standard: the Word of God."

26. Bremmer, "Schilder," 318.

27. K. Schilder, "Het Oordeel Begint van het Huis Gods," in Schilder, *Verzamelde Werken: Preken,* 1:183–84.

28. K. Schilder, "De Nieuwe Assemblée" (The New Assembly), in K. Schilder, *Verzamelde Werken, Afdeling II: Schriftoverdenkingen* (Collected Works, Section II: Meditations) (Goes: Oosterbaan & Le Cointre, 1958), 3:409.

29. The Doleantie was the movement of 1886, led by A. Kuyper, Sr., to free local churches from the liberal Dutch Reformed hierarchy.

30. On the union of 1892 and the refusal to join of some Christelijk Gereformeerde churches, see H. Bouma, *De Vereniging van 1892* (The Union of 1892) (Groningen: De Vuurbaak, 1967).

31. See K. Schilder, "Mélange," *De Bazuin* 71, no. 23 (1923): 3.

32. Cf. C. Trimp, "De Kerk bij A. Kuyper en K. Schilder," 193: "[Schilder was] . . . the man who had come to know the 'glorious breadth' of Christ's church, and who longed for it with his whole heart."

33. See K. Schilder, "Accentverlegging" (Moving the Accent), *De Bazuin* 71, no. 26 (1923): 3.

34. K. Schilder, "Over Interkerkelijkheid" (About Interdenominationalism), *Verzamelde Werken: De Kerk,* 1:62.

35. See Schilder's objections to H. Hoeksema's attempt to make binding a theology of the covenant "with the elect alone," in K. Schilder, *Bovenschriftuurlijke Binding —Een Nieuw Gevaar* (Binding Above Scripture—a New Danger) (Goes: van der Linden, n.d. [1952]).

36. K. Schilder, *Geen Duimbreed! Een Synodaal Besluit Inzake 't Lidmaatschap van N.S.B. en C.D.U.* (Not Even an Inch! A Synodical Decision Regarding Membership in the National Socialist Movement and the Christian Democratic Union) (Kampen: Kok, n.d. [1936]).

37. J. M. Batteau, "De Theologie van Abraham Kuyper: een Beoordeling" (The Theology of Abraham Kuyper: An Evaluation), *Radix* 13, no. 4 (1987): 218.

38. Cf. J. Douma, *Algemene Genade. Uiteenzetting, Vergelijking en Beoordeling van de Opvattingen van A. Kuyper, K. Schilder, en J. Calvijn over "Algemene Genade"* (Common Grace: Exposition, Comparison, and Evaluation of the Views of A. Kuyper, K. Schilder, and J. Calvin on 'Common Grace') (Goes: Oosterbaan & Le Cointre, 1976), 11–118. See also N. H. Gootjes, "Schilder on Christ and Culture," which forms chap. 3 in the present collection.

39. This was the source of contention between the Secession and the Doleantie factions of the united church after 1892, but it was resolved to some degree when H. Bavinck chose to teach at the Free University in 1902.

40. The general synod of the Reformed Churches in the Netherlands of 1905 deleted the words containing this statement.

41. For a more detailed description of Kuyper's ecclesiology, see P. A. van Leeuwen, *Het Kerkbegrip in de Theologie van Abraham Kuyper* (The Concept of Church in the Theology of Abraham Kuyper) (Franeker, The Netherlands: Wever, 1946).

42. The general doctrine of "immediate regeneration," without Kuyper's "organic" elaborations, was upheld by many Reformed scholars and theologians in the seventeenth century over against the Lutherans, who maintained that God always works "through" the Word. The Reformed emphasized the necessity of the Word *and* the sovereignty of the Spirit, often using the term *immediate* to speak of the Spirit's work in regenerating. The need for regeneration was apparent to them from the need for regeneration of infants and mentally retarded people, as well as from the fact that some people who hear the Word are not regenerated and others are. According to them, the Spirit always works in the sphere of the Word but is not always *dependent* on the Word. See H. Heppe, *Reformed Dogmatics, Set Out and Illustrated from the Sources,* trans. G. T. Thomson (Grand Rapids: Eerdmans, 1978), 521.

43. Cf. A. Kuyper, *De Gemene Gratie. Het Practisch Gedeelte* (Common Grace. The Practical Part) (Kampen: Kok, n.d. [1902–5]), 3:232–38. See also van Leeuwen, *Kerkbegrip Kuyper,* 201–36.

44. Cf. F. L. Rutgers, *De Geldigheid van de Oude Kerkenordening der Nederlandsche Gereformeerde Kerken* (The Validity of the Old Church Order of the Reformed Churches in the Netherlands) (Amsterdam: Wormser, 1890).

45. That is, the Nederlandse Christelijke Radio Vereeniging, which, translated, is the Dutch Christian Radio Society.

46. Cf. W. G. de Vries, "K. Schilder in Zijn Hantering en Waardering van de Gereformeerde Confessie" (K. Schilder in his Use of and Appreciation for the Reformed Confession), in Douma et al., eds., *K. Schilder: Aspecten,* 40–42.

47. Cf. W. G. de Vries, *Calvinisten op de Tweesprong: De Internationale Federatie van Calvinisten en haar Invloed op de onderlinge Verhoudingen in De Gereformeerde Kerken in Nederland in de Dertiger Jaren van de Twintigste Eeuw* (Calvinists at Crossroads: The International Federation of Calvinists and Its Influence on the Mutual Relationships in the Reformed Churches in the Netherlands in the Thirties of the Twentieth Century) (Groningen: De Vuurbaak, 1974).

48. Cf. Smit, "Gehoorzamen," 76.

49. For Ten Hoor's views, see F. M. Ten Hoor, *Afscheiding en Doleantie in Verband met het Kerkbegrip* (Secession and Doleantie in Connection with the Church Concept) (Leiden: Donner, 1890); and *Afscheiding of Doleantie: Een Woord tot Verdediging en Nadere Toelichting* (Secession or Doleantie: A Word of Defense and Further Explanation) (Leiden: Donner, 1891).

50. Cf. Smit, "Gehoorzamen," 74–75.

51. Schilder, *Verzamelde Werken: De Kerk,* 2:202.

52. Schilder, *Verzamelde Werken: De Kerk,* 2:203–4.

53. With respect to the agreement of the Reformed creeds on the authority of Scripture, see J. Kamphuis, *In Dienst van de Vrede: De Kerkelijke Consensus als Dogmatische Factor* (In the Service of Peace: Ecclesiastical Consensus as Dogmatic Factor) (Groningen: De Vuurbaak, 1979), 53–54.

54. Heppe, *Reformed Dogmatics*, 657–94.

55. G. C. Berkouwer, in Berkouwer, *The Church. Studies in Dogmatics,* 19–20, laments the fact that Schilder's "view is often seen as a certain form of churchism [*kerkisme*], where one has eye only for one's own Church."

56. J. Kamphuis, "Critische Sympathie over den Dogmatischen Arbeid van Dr. K. Schilder" (Critical Appreciation for K. Schilder's Work in Dogmatics), in *Almanak van het Corpus Studiosorum in Academia Campensi, "Fides Quadrat Intellectum"* (Kampen: Zalsman, 1953), 73–89.

57. Kamphuis, "Critische Sympathie," 89.

58. For a discussion of this issue see Richard A. Muller, *Post-Reformation Reformed Dogmatics,* vol. 1. *Prolegomena to Theology* (Grand Rapids: Baker, 1987), 13–40.

59. See, for example, Calvin on God's covenant with Abraham in his commentary on Gen. 12 to 17. Calvin distinguishes there between the *covenant relation* and *eternal election*. Commenting on Gen. 17:7 (". . . I will establish my covenant between me and you and your descendants after you . . ."), Calvin says, "There is no doubt that the Lord distinguishes the race of Abraham from the rest of the world. . . . Now they are deceived who think that his elect alone are here pointed out . . ." (John Calvin, *Commentary on the First Book of Moses Called*

Genesis, trans. J. King [Grand Rapids: Baker, 1979 (reprint)], 447). See also J. van Genderen, *Verbond en Verkiezing* (Covenant and Election) (Kampen: Kok, 1983), 77–79, and J. M. Batteau, "The Covenant in Reformed Theology: Some Key Moments (1)," *Lux Mundi* 6, no. 1 (1987): 9–11.

60. K. Schilder, *Looze Kalk: Een Wederwoord over de Zedelijke Crisis in de "Gereformeerde Kerken in Nederland"* (Untempered Mortar: A Response About the Ethical Crisis in the Reformed Churches in the Netherlands) (Groningen: De Jager, 1946), 14–20. See also K. Schilder, "In het Verbond Komen of er al in Zijn: Calvijn's Gebed" (Coming into the Covenant or Being in it Already: Calvin's Prayer), *De Reformatie* 24, no. 4 (1948): 32–33.

61. K. Dijk, *"Buiten de Kerk Geen Zaligheid": Artikel 27–29 der Nederlandsche Geloofsbelijdenis* ("There Is No Salvation Outside the Church": Articles 27–29 of the Belgic Confession) (Amsterdam: Kirchner, n.d. [1920]). See also van Leeuwen, *Kerkbegrip Kuyper,* 230.

62. G. Doekes, *De Moeder der Geloovigen: "Onzer aller Moeder"* (The Mother of the Believers: "The Mother of Us All") (Nijverdal: Bosch, n.d. [1909]). See particularly chap. 3, "De Ware Kerk" (The True Church), 40–51.

63. Heppe, *Reformed Dogmatics,* 661. See H. Bavinck, *Our Reasonable Faith. A Survey of Christian Doctrine,* trans. H. Zylstra (Grand Rapids: Baker, 1977 [reprint]), 521. The title of the original Dutch work was *Magnalia Dei.*

64. Schilder, *De Kerk. College-dictaat,* 21.

65. Ibid., 21.

66. Ibid., 22.

67. *De Reformatie* 18, nos. 34–37 (1935); see also Schilder, *De Kerk. College-dictaat,* 123–25, and Schilder, *Verzamelde Werken: De Kerk,* 2:245–50; for an English translation see *The Canadian Reformed Magazine* 21, no. 17 (1972), and *Clarion* 24, no. 15 (1975).

68. We find similar words in a polemic that Schilder carried on in 1929: "In our day there is a desire on the part of those who are not Reformed to construct the concept of the church from experience, from what is observable, from what appears to be realizable. This is to apply the rationalistic, modern method of reasoning to the church. No, the church is a matter of faith. . . . In describing the being of the church I have nothing to do with empirical states of affairs or with the practical situation of what is achievable, but only with special revelation, the Word of God . . ." (quoted in J. Kamphuis, "Critische Sympathie," 86).

69. Heppe, *Reformed Dogmatics,* 660.

70. Ibid.

71. Question and Answer 54: "What do you believe concerning the *holy catholic Christian church?* I believe that the Son of God, out of the whole human race, from the beginning of the world to its end, gathers, defends, and preserves for Himself, by His Spirit and Word, in the unity of the true faith, a church chosen to everlasting life . . ." (*Book of Praise,* 495).

5

SCHILDER ON HEAVEN[1]

J. Kamphuis

Schilder's *What Is Heaven?* (1935)[2] is a dogmatic treatise character-ized by a compelling harmony.[3] A song rises from this treatise owing to "the profound happiness" of being allowed to reflect in a Reformed manner on God's glory in the consummation of His works. It is hard to describe this hymn-like dogmatic treatise. The book has to be read as a whole: in the progression of thought each part reflects the whole. Such a composition cannot be condensed into a few pages. Whoever tries to portray the grandeur of a Gothic cathedral by building a min-iature with building blocks makes himself ridiculous. A cathedral needs space; its beholder, time to contemplate it. Therefore, in what follows I do not attempt to summarize. Instead I wish to draw attention to a number of points, merely as an introduction to this book.

    1. *What Is Heaven?*—Schilder's first thetic-dogmatic publica-tion after becoming a professor in 1934—occupies a central place in his work. It presents the results of his confrontation with the dialectic theology, while focusing on the theme of history and eschatology. It introduces themes that will continue to appear in later publications, especially in his commentary on the Heidelberg Catechism: the con-fession about the Trinity, God's counsel, the covenant, the Word spo-ken to us in its indissoluble correlation of promise and demand, the

issue of so-called common grace, and so on. All these themes are discussed in *What Is Heaven?* in a concentrated but obvious way. Whoever has gained access to this work has an introduction to all of Schilder's theology.

2. Without compromise Schilder makes his starting point the faith in Scripture, specifically in the historical trustworthiness of the history related in Genesis 2 and 3, dealing with the original state of righteousness and the fall into sin. In this book Schilder does not refer even once to the decisions of the Synod of Assen of 1926[4] regarding the historical trustworthiness of the narrative in Genesis 2 and 3.[5] Nevertheless, Berkouwer's words are strikingly applicable to *What Is Heaven?* "I know of no theologian within the circle of Reformed theology for whom the decision of Assen was of more material significance than it was for Schilder."[6] Schilder reminds us repeatedly of his position: "With respect to the *beginning* of the world we must accept the historicity of the narrative of Genesis 1–3."[7] This is *the* starting point.[8] Schilder frankly concedes the existence of a fundamental antithesis in this matter: "Do you not believe . . . in a state of righteousness? If not, then between you and us lies *Scripture*."[9] In this Schilder didn't budge an inch! In 1935 these words were directed particularly against the spokesmen for dialectical theology and those who fully or partially supported them. But they have lost none of their force today.[10] While Schilder advances the proposition that "it is only on earth that we can think of heaven"[11] in order to bind himself and everyone else to the "revelation given from above," Kuitert and others posit that "revelation itself is a word from below about above."[12] This means that Schilder has already taken a position *against* any kind of theology of experience in his theology of revelation—revelation coming from above and demanding faith. Here the ways part. At the same time it may be said that the Reformed belief in the Scriptures[13] never has demonstrated its vitality more convincingly and more beautifully than in *What Is Heaven?* Whoever disqualifies this belief in the Scriptures as fundamentalism after having read *What Is Heaven?* hands himself a certificate of spiritual and theological incompetence.

3. Schilder, again in opposition to dialectical theology, wrote about heaven, starting from his belief in the unity of history. There-

fore, in the second chapter of *What Is Heaven?* he explicitly made a stand in opposition to this theology. His concern was with the unity and the value of history: "History, as well, is a work of God,"[14] "a frame for God's work, . . . it is itself God's work."[15] The captivating effect of *What Is Heaven?* derives from the fact that Schilder dares to pull heaven out of a static immovable sphere, and that he sees heaven, too, taken up in the framework of history. Protology (the doctrine of the first things) and eschatology (the doctrine of the last things) are thus conceived from the same perspective. It is important that Schilder, by speaking about heaven completely in the frame of history, was able to disengage himself also from "the desire for distinctions" of Protestant dogmatics "that pulled the heavenly spheres apart, placing one statically opposite another, fixing heaven itself in a static distance opposite the earth, thus separating what God draws together and causes to affect each other."[16] We meet this same dynamic-historical thinking of Schilder with reference to the church; it opposes every desire for distinctions (visible-invisible, militant-triumphant, and so on): "Such criteria of classification that do not take into consideration the (church) *gathering* factor are the cause of many misunderstandings concerning the church."[17]

4. When Schilder criticizes Protestant dogmatics because of its "failure to recognize the element of history,"[18] he addresses in the first place *Reformed* dogmatics, that of the sixteenth and seventeenth centuries and that of the nineteenth and twentieth centuries (Kuyper and Bavinck). But it must be added that no matter how critical Schilder may have been of his own tradition, it was and remained fully his own background, and he himself was clearly conscious of this. The dialectical understanding of eschatology (that which does not belong to this world but has a different history, and which only momentarily grazes our history like a straight line grazes the outer edge of a circle) is demarcated from eschatology "in the *old,* and for us so familiar, meaning," which we need to retain,[19] namely, as referring to the doctrine of "the *eschata,* the last things, the last things *in history,* the *final* act of history."[20] When we hold Schilder's position here next to what he said about the doctrine of the first things, we see that Schilder's thinking, beginning with the unity of Creation and re-creation and with his acceptance of the trustworthiness of Scripture with respect to

the state of righteousness, is aligned very clearly with Reformed tradition. A look at H. Bavinck's chapter on the state of righteousness in his *Gereformeerde Dogmatiek* clearly supports this. I quote just one passage: "Thus, Adam stood not at the end, but at the beginning of the road; his situation was temporary and temporal, it could not remain as it was, and had to go on to either a higher glory or a fall into sin and death."[21]

5. However, the originality of Schilder's thinking strikes us when we see him join this "going on to the higher glory" with the (for him all-important) "shock" idea[22] in line with 1 Corinthians 15: the carrying over of this changing world into the world of the consummation. The convergence in Schilder's thought of the gradual development of the world since Creation and of the transformation of this world into the coming world by a shock movement distinguishes his position from all evolutionism and horizontal cultural optimism. God intervenes sovereignly and transcendentally. He will intervene at the end of history just as He did in the course of the days of Creation. He will make something new (*chedasjah*).[23] This was already a perspective in Paradise. In my opinion, Schilder jumps here repeatedly from what is structural, so to speak, for God's work, to what man knows of it already in Paradise. To cite one of the many instances: "Man in Paradise then shut the idea of his (that is, man's) *carrying* the old into the new out of his heart. And it stayed out, as long as he was without sin."[24] We must distinguish, however, between the knowledge of faith and God's revelation in His Word and in His works! Though we may question Schilder on this point, we must not loose sight of the intention and substance of his argument: man may and must cooperate with God on God's way to the end, although man remains dependent on God and on His sovereign intervention.

6. Schilder was persistent in taking his starting point in protology whenever he dealt with eschatology: "Everything that follows must be explained in light of the *beginning;* only then is it possible to see where the trends are going in the *end*."[25] This is where the intention of his theology becomes visible. The issue for Schilder concerns that which is *structural*. This is also the core of his opposition to the idea of common grace, namely, that in this way "that which was still left after the fall"[26] would be the deciding factor for our thinking.

7. Schilder's thought has a theocentric-Christological character.

Theocentric: Man began as an office bearer. "In the idea of office we see God's primeval right to man."[27] Thus it was with respect to protology.[28] As far as eschatology is concerned, the triune God brings all creation to its consummate glory by virtue of the *pactum salutis* (His covenant of peace).[29] Schilder again sings the praises of the Reformed tradition in which he wishes to stand, and his song is not due to prejudice, but to wonderment: "Reformed theology began to consider these things long ago. She was predestined to do so; she alone knew what it meant: to climb up to God with everything."[30]

Christological: "Reformed dogmatics must do everything possible to remain faithful to the thought that Christ did not come to do something entirely new in a 'second history,' but to save what God purposed *from the very beginning*";[31] after this comes the confession of Christ's passion: He bore the penalty for our sins. But this confession is tied to the confession of Christ's "active obedience": He "took up the line of history again [as this began before the fall into sin with the covenant of 'works'] where Adam did not keep it in his hands."[32] Therefore, it is "Christ *and* culture," because Christ in His suffering presented to the Father His passive and active obedience.

8. Even when one knows himself to be united with Schilder in his belief in the Scriptures, this does not mean that there are no critical questions to be posed. Unfortunately, this criticism has often taken the form of caricature. Thus, I do not believe that Schilder meant to portray heaven as a region of "cold static rigidness"[33] when he described "heaven," or rather "God's dwelling place with man" in the consummation, as the *fulfillment* of history. When Schilder states that in the consummation resting and working "[have] become identical,"[34] this does not mean that working will have *ceased.* Schilder says that in heaven there is no longer this always again *coming* but also always again *being gone* of the feasts of the old and new covenants: "In heaven all this is abolished, *because* it is fulfilled. There the servant is lord, just in his serving; there the one who asks is, just in his asking, rich with goods; and all is encompassed in the eternal year of jubilee."[35] I get the impression that such criticism—the caricature of Schilder's view as one of "cold static rigidness"—has problems understanding the word *fulfillment,* the fulfillment of God's works

by Himself. In contrast with this criticism, a bath in the theology of
Schilder, the theology of expectation, is refreshing. It has often been
overlooked that Schilder took great pains to understand the reality of
the fulfillment and to give it expression in a concrete way,[36] at the
same time recognizing that he had reached the limits of human understanding: "Here every pen refuses to go on. We are unable to go any
further."[37]

But this does not mean that we may not ask the question of
whether Schilder has not already gone too far. This is the more so
since he repeatedly asserts that "the new world" will in no way know
any development. He uses the verb *to bloom:* "Nature there will
bloom." But he immediately relativizes this blooming by emphasizing the completed state of God's work in history. "Again we have
said too much. . . . What is 'blooming' in a new world, which knows
no becoming, no growing. . . ."[38] At first sight this seems to be a
cautious statement, but in reality it is extremely bold! And Schilder
even applies it integrally to man. Schilder has Scripture behind him
when he says that the vegetal and sexual aspects of life will have
fulfilled their service (an important word in this context). However,
from this it does not follow that man's *office* before God will no longer
experience any development in the coming world. Schilder was cap-
tivated by Lord's Day 12 of the Heidelberg Catechism, which deals
with the offices both of Christ and of the Christian who lives in com-
munion with his Lord. But he did not pay enough attention to the
final words of this confession, in which the Christian, looking at Christ
in faith, confesses concerning himself, ". . . that I may . . . after this
life, reign with him eternally over all creatures." Here the texts of
Scripture are also clear (2 Tim. 2:12 and Rev. 22:5). But in Schilder's
thought these texts do not function. Schilder was correct in drawing
attention to the fulfillment of history, but he was incorrect when he
thought that he was allowed to make this fulfillment concrete only in
the Son's presentation of the faithful to the Father: "And look, now
He in turn gives them to the Father, in order that the kingdom may be
the Lord's."[39] This is related to Schilder's difficulty in ascribing to
Christ, "the Lamb," his rightful position in God's fulfilled kingdom
of glory.[40] And this in turn is connected to his difficulty with the relationship between the economic Trinity and the ontological Trinity.[41]

In Schilder's eschatology the economic Trinity has been assimilated, as it were, into the ontological Trinity, the Trinity in its essence. At the very least, this tendency is present as a threat. In the theology since Schleiermacher, the ontological Trinity has tended to give way to the "so-called"[42] economic Trinity—imposing a fatal wound to the doctrine and life of faith—but the opposite tendency is present in Schilder's theology. I say "tendency" because Schilder does say elsewhere "that the *preservation* of the world shall be the work of the triune God for eternity."[43] And this preserving of creation is fully the work of the God who *reveals* Himself in His works as the triune God because He *is* the triune One. But even such a formulation as the one just cited is conspicuously meager, especially for Schilder. For he constantly warned against abstracting God's preserving from His *governing:* God's preserving is subservient to His governing. Why then does he say nothing of God's *governing* in the coming world? Is it because he cannot imagine what purpose such a governing would serve? Is that why he says nothing about man's rule over all creation with Christ? But—though we must wait for the coming world for concrete knowledge (1 John 3:2)—will not the glory of God remain God's own purpose for all eternity, and the purpose of those who with Christ share in the *munus,* the office, of ruling all things? We may not know how, but we confess the fact thereof, and it raises our expectation. This also makes room for the biblical notions of an inheritance and of heirs.[44]

9. But this criticism does not take away our thankfulness for Schilder's contribution to Christian thought in *What Is Heaven?* It is here that one really learns to be aware of "horizontalism," and to "remain faithful to the earth" in a truly Christian manner, which is not the manner prescribed by Nietzsche through the mouth of Zarathustra. In eschatological expectation, Schilder proclaimed the value of history. Therein lies the contemporary importance of his message. He saw *all* things enclosed in history as the framework of God's activity. "It is *impossible* to conceive of man apart from the cosmos. *From the beginning* God saw and placed man in relation to the entire cosmos, and thus he *remains* in this relationship."[45] Therefore, the lack of eschatological expectation is "a violation of this created life. It is a sin, not only against God, but also against man, and against the cosmos."[46]

On this point this dogmatic treatise of the 1930s has its relevance at the end of the twentieth century, which is confronted with the essential questions of how to deal with the earth and with life itself. Here the Reformed belief in the Scriptures retains its relevance for our time. Consequently, those who believe the Scriptures retain their calling to address these questions of their own time and to tackle contemporary issues courageously and honestly. Schilder remains a forerunner herein almost forty years after his death. *Facing the Scriptures,* he called for a decision. From there he pointed to the way leading across *this* earth and through our history to *the* future. He sought and saw distant perspectives; his heart was delighted, and he delighted the heart of God's congregation. Even when we have our critical questions for Schilder on the basis of our common starting point, our belief in the Scriptures, we shall never forget that this delight was not the result of a fata morgana. The covenant reaches its fulfillment when God's dwelling place comes to be with man; that is, all covenant is fulfilled: the "covenant of works,'" the "covenant of grace," the "covenant of nature," and God's "covenant of peace."[47] Thus also the Sabbath is fulfilled, the guarantee of cultural-historical peace and of cosmic peace.[48] Again, perspectives are opened before us! We had no intelligent fantast, no dreamer, but a prophetic seer in the midst of the congregation of Pentecost.

Notes

1. Throughout this essay *Wat is de Hemel?* (Kampen: Kok, 1935) is translated *What Is Heaven?* M. M. Schooland calls his abridged English translation *Heaven, What Is It?* (Grand Rapids: Eerdmans, 1950). Whenever passages cited from *Wat is de Hemel?* occur also in this English version, page numbers in the latter are preceded by slashes.
2. I refer to the second edition, published in Kampen in 1954; the first appeared in 1935. It was Schilder's intention that the second edition be a "revised edition." He wished to apply "corrections" and "make a few limited additions to the text," according to the "concept-preface" of the second edition, which was published after his death by P. A. C. Schilder in 1953. The latter writes, "The author revised the first chapter and part of the second; he also made a few notes elsewhere in the text, and the present corrector has attempted to take these into account. Thus, this reprint can 'boast' to be a partial revision. In substance, however, there are no differences." This latter statement proves true when the two editions are carefully compared.

3. Schilder states emphatically that *What Is Heaven?* is a "book for laymen," and that it is not set up according to scientific principles (p. 69). But even when this is taken into account, the fact remains that Schilder, in relatively little space, managed to present a number of central theological themes in such a way that the reader is impressed by the harmonious structure of the work.

4. Editor's note: The 1926 Synod of Assen of the Reformed Churches in the Netherlands (GKN) dealt with objections to the teachings of Dr. J. G. Geelkerken, which undermined the historical trustworthiness of Gen. 1–3; the Synod maintained this historical trustworthiness.

5. Schilder does allude to the Synod of Assen of 1926 elsewhere, for example, in K. Schilder, *Christ and Culture,* trans. G. Van Rongen and W. Helder (Winnipeg: Premier, 1977): "The paradise-reality, including the first Adam, is by no means a so-called 'higher' reality [the tendency opposed by Assen]; it is simply *undefiled* reality, though in all other respects it is very concrete, temporal, matter of fact, real historical, containing flesh and blood as well as soul and spirit. And Spirit" (p. 39). In K. Schilder, *Heidelbergsche Catechismus* (4 vols. [Goes: Oosterbaan & Le Cointre, 1947–51]), he writes concerning the tree of the knowledge of good and evil, "We are surely dealing here with a 'tree,' more precisely with a 'forbidden' tree. Now a tree is a sensorially perceptible thing ['sensorially perceptible' is *the* key term of Assen!]; but as soon as it becomes '*forbidden,*' it appears in a judicial-legal context and in the relation to obedience and trust or to disobedience and unbelief" (1:322).

6. G. C. Berkouwer, *Zoeken en Vinden. Herinneringen en Ervaringen* (Seeking and Finding. Memories and Experiences) (Kampen: Kok, 1989), 265. Evidently Berkouwer was preoccupied with Schilder's positive adherence to Assen (see pp. 238, 265, and 298). Berkouwer himself, however, took a totally different stance: see especially G. C. Berkouwer, *Dogmatische Studien. De Heilige Schrift* (Kampen: Kok, 1967), 2:295–323. (Editor's note: See also the much-abbreviated English translation by J. B. Rogers, *Holy Scripture* [Grand Rapids: Eerdmans, 1975], 292–95). It is inconceivable that the decision taken by the "synodical" Reformed Churches at the Synod of Amsterdam in 1967, "that the doctrinal decision, namely of Assen, 1926, shall no longer be in force in the churches as a doctrinal decision," was not influenced by Berkouwer.

7. Schilder, *Wat is de Hemel?* 50. The emphasis on the authority of God's revelation is slightly stronger in the second edition of *What Is Heaven?* than in the first edition. The first edition says, "No other path to knowledge has been opened than the one opened by revelation." The second edition reads, "No other path to knowledge has been opened than the one opened by the *revelation* given from above."

8. Schilder chooses this starting point because he is convinced that the testimony of Scripture concerning itself should be accepted; in Gen. 2 and 3 Scripture presents itself as history. See W. H. Gispen, *Genesis* (Kampen: Kok, 1974), 1:91: "Both the creation narrative and the narrative of Gen. 2 and 3 form part of the book of Genesis. Genesis presents itself as historical narrative, evidenced

by its chronological order as well as its genealogies, and it is remarkable that there is no distinct partition between chapters 11 and 12, between the 'pre-history' and the history of the patriarchs, Abraham, Isaac, and Jacob." Notice that Gispen presents exegetical considerations and is not judging *a prima vista.* Cf. Berkouwer, *Dogmatische Studien. De Heilige Schrift,* 2:312.

9. Schilder, *Wat is de Hemel?,* 51; similarly, p. 54. This basic antithesis dominates Schilder's theology, for example, in Schilder, *Heidelbergsche Catechismus,* 1:250, with reference to the doctrine of the image of God, and in Schilder, *Verzamelde Werken. Part II. Schriftoverdenkingen* (Collected Works. Part II. Meditations) (Goes: Oosterbaan & Le Cointre, 1958), 3:573, in opposition to Karl Barth regarding election and reprobation, and the death of Christ as the counterpart to His resurrection.

10. This must be said also concerning J. Veenhof, "Medewerkers van God. K. Schilder over Plaats en Taak van de Mens in het Handelen van God" (Coworkers with God. K. Schilder Concerning Man's Place and Task in the Work of God), in W. F. de Gaay Fortman et al., eds., *"Achter den Tijd. Opstellen Aangeboden aan Dr. G. Puchinger ter Gelegenheid van zijn Vijfenzestigste Verjaardag* (Behind the Times. Essays Presented to Dr. G. Puchinger on the Occasion of His Sixty-fifth Birthday) (Haarlem: Aca-Media, 1986), 151–52.

11. Schilder, *Wat is de Hemel?* 19/16.

12. H. M. Kuitert, *Wat Heet Geloven? Struktuur en Herkomst van Christelijke Geloofsuitspraken* (What Is Called Believing? Structure and Origin of Christian Pronouncements of Faith) (Baarn: Ten Have, 1977), 155.

13. We purposely use this term (Dutch *Schriftgeloof*) to show how close the bond was between the exegete S. Greijdanus and K. Schilder; see also J. Kamphuis, "Het Gereformeerd Karakter van het 'Schriftgeloof' van Prof. Dr. S. Greijdanus" (The Reformed Character of Prof. Dr. S. Greijdanus's "Belief in the Scriptures"), in *Altijd met Goed Accoord* (Always in Good Harmony) (Amsterdam: Ton Bolland, 1973), 85–96. Greijdanus's influence on Schilder has not been sufficiently examined and recognized.

14. Schilder, *Wat is de Hemel?* 221/112.

15. Ibid, 86/39.

16. Ibid., 81.

17. From Schilder's fifteenth proposition (p. 93, above) concerning the church; see K. Schilder, *Verzamelde Werken. De Kerk* (Collected Works. The Church) (Goes: Oosterbaan & Le Cointre, 1962), 2:245–50. The quotation is from p. 249.

18. Schilder, *Wat is de Hemel?* 81.

19. Ibid., 53.

20. Ibid., 20; similarly, p. 50.

21. H. Bavinck, *Gereformeerde Dogmatiek* (Kampen: Kok, 1928), vol. 2, par. 38, "De Bestemming van den Mensch" (The Destination of Man). The quotation is from p. 526. The Scripture proofs are identical to those of Schilder. See, for example, p. 525: "There is an immense difference between the physical and the pneumatical, between the *status integritatis* (state of righteousness) and the

status gloriae (state of glory). Digestion and food will be done away with after the resurrection (1 Cor. 6:13), but Adam had both; the children of God will no longer marry in heaven, but shall be like the angels (Matt. 22:30), and yet Adam needed the help of a woman."

22. Schilder, *Wat is de Hemel?* 92/43; similarly, p. 33.

23. Ibid., 95/46.

24. Ibid., 217/111; similarly, p. 93/44.

25. Ibid., 206/107; similarly, p. 86/39.

26. Ibid., 206/107.

27. Ibid.

28. Anthropology also can be discussed within the framework of protology. It is important—not just for a good assessment of Schilder—to realize that *anthropological* questions can be dealt with *theocentrically* on the basis of the idea of office. This is the importance of the doctrine concerning the image of God.

29. Editor's note: the term *pactum salutis* ("covenant of peace") means the eternal covenant between Father, Son, and Spirit, in which the three divine persons "agreed together" to create, to save, and to sanctify and glorify the chosen people for living with God on the new earth, in the New Jerusalem.

30. Schilder, *Wat is de Hemel?* 190; similarly, p. 149.

31. Ibid., 97.

32. Ibid.

33. C. van der Waal, *Openbaring van Jezus Christus* (Revelation of Jesus Christ) (Oudkarspel: De Nijverheid, 1981), 2:379. For the refutation of this criticism see J. Kamphuis, "Het Lam en het Nieuwe Jeruzalem" (The Lamb and the New Jerusalem), in *Almanak Fides Quadrat Intellectum 1987* (Kampen: Zalsman, 1987), 211, 223 nn. 33, 34.

34. Schilder, *Wat is de Hemel?* 201/104, 231/117.

35. Ibid., 201.

36. Thus O. Jager, "Concretiseren tot het Uiterste" (Being Concrete to the Extreme), in G. Puchinger, ed., *Ontmoetingen met Schilder* (Encounters with Schilder) (Kampen: Kok, 1990), 63.

37. Ibid., 231/118.

38. Ibid., 221.

39. Ibid., 192/98; similarly, pp. 170, 149.

40. See J. Kamphuis, "Het Lam."

41. Editor's note: this distinction occurs, in fact, also in articles 8 and 9 of the Belgic Confession. In article 8 we confess the ontological Trinity: "We believe in one only God, who is one *in essence,* in which are three persons. . . ." In the last paragraph of article 9 we confess the economic Trinity: "We must observe *the distinct offices and works of these three Persons toward us. . . ,*" dealing with the triune God as He reveals and gives Himself to us in His works "towards us." For these terms see L. Berkhof, *Systematic Theology* (Grand Rapids: Eerdmans, 1941), 88–89.

42. Editor's note: "so-called" is added here by the author to indicate that what Schleiermacher and other liberal theologians mean by the term "economic Trinity" or "revelation Trinity" is far different from what Reformed theologians mean by it.

43. Schilder, *Heidelbergsche Catechismus,* 2:89.

44. The inheritance (1 Peter 1:4–5), the Son as heir (Heb. 1:2), the children of God as coheirs (Rom. 8:17; similarly Matt. 5:5). See also Rom. 4:13 (Abraham as heir of the world). C. van der Waal's narrowing of "world" to "land" is justly rejected by H. van de Kamp in *Israel in Openbaring. Een Onderzoek naar de Plaats van het Joodse Volk in het Toekomstbeeld van de Openbaring aan Johannes* (Israel in Revelation. An Investigation into the Place of the Jewish People in the Future in the Revelation to John), diss. (Kampen: Kok, 1990), 92, 193, 195n.63, 292n.80. In the latter passage van de Kamp agrees "with a view held by exegetes of the first centuries, that the holy city is the land that was promised to the patriarchs and that it encompasses the world."

45. Schilder, *Wat is de Hemel?,* 228.

46. Ibid., 68/28; similarly, p. 106/54.

47. Ibid., 172–94/85–99.

48. Ibid., 204–31/106–18.

6

SCHILDER ON REVELATION

J. De Jong

This paper is a commemoration of the work of Dr. K. Schilder. It is always precarious to remember people rather than events. For one runs the risk of glorifying something in man, or man himself, rather than boasting only in the Lord. Idolizing individuals hardly illustrates sound living in the church. Yet we can be thankful for what the Lord has given in this many-faceted theologian and scholar who played such an important role in the recent history of the church in the Netherlands. Scripture says, "Remember your leaders, those who spoke to you the word of God; consider the outcome of their life and imitate their faith" (Heb. 13:7). It is in light of this verse that this commemoration should be understood.

Elsewhere in this book the reader will find data on Schilder's life and work. For our purposes it is important to note that Schilder's work represents an ongoing exchange with the leading philosophical and theological ideas of his day. Although his early publications show a mastery of a wide range of literature on national and international levels, it was particularly his doctoral dissertation that marked him as a scholar of international caliber.[1] Schilder received a number of study leaves for his doctoral studies, and he lived in Erlangen between the First and Second World Wars, a time of great flux in Germany. Visiting Berlin and Munich, he witnessed the rise of the national socialist movement, and so became very familiar with the fundamental principles underlying this movement. He traced the origin of national socialism to a revival of themes from ancient pagan German religions, from the nihilist philosophy of Friedrich Wilhelm Nietzsche (1844–1900), and from the philosophy of Georg Wilhelm Friedrich Hegel (1770–1831). Hegel held the state to be the Divine Idea as it exists on the earth—a dominant theme in Nazi propaganda. All of these exposures brought Schilder into contact with the leading figures in the history of European thought.

This is of great significance for the central battle of Schilder's career, that concerning God's revelation. One's view of the revelation of God concerns the starting point of all theology, and on this starting point one stands or falls. The struggle of that time on the point of revelation and the Scriptures was very intense. Schilder referred to it as the major battle of his time.[2] In this chapter we want to look at two basic points in this battle: (1) the essentials of the struggle in Schilder's time and (2) the abiding significance of this struggle for today.

Schilder grew up in a time of immense intellectual upheaval. Some of this was imported from Germany, but Holland itself was also in ferment. The younger generation was somewhat dissatisfied and impatient with positions that had become the status quo in the church, namely, the position reflected in the intellectual heritage of A. Kuyper and H. Bavinck. Already in 1920 cracks were noticeable in the huge intellectual edifice built by the great theologian and statesman Abraham Kuyper and perpetuated by his immediate followers and their students. Kuyperian thought ruled the day, but it was a building unsuited to changing patterns of the twentieth-century world. Kuyper had worked extensively with the scholastic categories of late Reformed orthodoxy. But the emerging century was fundamentally antischolastic in thought and direction.

At the same time, dialectical theology began its surge to influence and fame in Switzerland, Germany, and surrounding countries. It was represented by two figures in particular, Karl Barth and Emil Brunner. For Barth the realization that he had to take a new direction came in August of 1914, when ninety-three leading intellectuals, among whom were some of his teachers, signed an open letter supporting the imperialist policies of the German emperor, Wilhelm II, and his counsellors. This, said Barth, was a result of the arrogance of the old school liberalism, which had made all religion into a mockery. In liberalism, the golden rule was love and tolerance, and Jesus was seen only as an example of this love. Religion was put into a form that would not offend anyone. The result was that no one dared to speak up against things that were wrong in the world and in the church. It was a way of looking at the world in which man made himself God.

So from Barth and others came a fierce and unrelenting attack on all the holy cows of the old liberal religion. Hardly anyone escaped his sharp and penetrating pen. In opposition to the soft and easy religion of the liberals Barth emphasized the transcendence of God, that is, His wrath, His holiness, and His glory. He maintained that God is the Wholly Other, and he accented God's incomprehensibility and inaccessibility. In fact, he stated, man cannot know God in his own power. God is the opposite of anything that can be known by man. Never can you get God in your intellectual control. Hence the term *dialectical* theology.

Literally the word *dialectical* means "saying things opposite to each other." For Barth, God was so great that one statement could never say anything fully true about Him. It always needed to be complemented with its opposite, and that statement, in turn, required its own opposite, and so on. Opposing statements form only an attempt to get at the truth. In his statements man may ask questions, but he can never expect *the* answer. Every church dogma is a question, an attempt, a search for the truth; dogmatic propositions thus aim at being on the way to the truth of revelation.[3]

What did Barth say about revelation? God reveals Himself, but this revelation is an event, an act. And it is never something that lasts so that it can be codified. It is always something that happens to you. Nothing you do can make it happen; like a lightning bolt flashing out of the sky, it happens only in God's time and in His good pleasure. To be sure, God uses the Bible and speaks through it. But the Bible itself is not revelation, nor is it the Word of God. It only *contains* the Word of God; or better, it is only a witness to God's revelation. It recalls past revelation and anticipates future revelation. But for Barth, it is a human document, written by fallible men. You must read it, and it must be preached. But these are all fallible and sinful actions, and the words are not God's words. He makes them His words when and how He wills—at His time, in His way, in a moment of time. This moment!—that is what is important in dialectical theology. God and the Bible are opposite poles, and yet they are poles that need each other! God is divine; the Bible is thoroughly human. Yet God at His time takes the words and thoughts of the Bible and transforms them into His speech for man. Here there is an overemphasis on the subjective element in revelation, that is, the human experience of God's speech. This is coupled with a corresponding depreciation of the objective element of revelation, that is, the words of Scripture.

Let us return to Holland. Of course, many of the ideas outlined above streamed down the Rhine and filtered into the Netherlands. But in the Reformed churches, the reigning perspective was that of Abraham Kuyper and his Calvinist principles (*beginselen*). This prolific author, statesman, and theologian had an elaborate view of divine revelation. He believed that all knowledge of God is suited to the form and measure of man.[4] God uses all kinds of means to implant His revelation in the minds of men. Yet fundamentally, through the Holy Spirit He speaks directly to the human self-consciousness.[5] This is the dominant element in Kuyper's thought. As C. Trimp puts it, the fundamental cornerstone of Kuyper's Calvinism was the immediate relationship of fellowship that God has with the believer through His Holy Spirit.[6] There would not have been any need for a written Bible in a world without sin. It was only our sin that brought on the necessity of God's putting the revelation of His will in writing. Kuyper said that having God's Word in writing is an added element in revelation that first appears after the Fall. To be sure, the Bible is the inspired Word of God. But the power and real force in inspiration is external to the text. It is a spiritual element added to a material element (the text), a divine element added to a human element; and the human element shows the weaknesses characteristic of humanity.[7] Kuyper often uses the image of a diamond. As a diamond is dull in itself, and its glitter only shines when a ray of light penetrates to its center, so also a clear, bright, and full effect only goes forth from

Holy Scripture when the Holy Spirit enlightens, unfolds, and applies it.[8] In his lecture notes we find these words:

> Scripture is a *medium gratiae* [medium of grace]. Just as the sacrament of baptism and the Lord's Supper. In themselves, these also are nothing. Water, bread, and wine are only symbols; but behind them there is a spiritual working, a mystery of God. So also in the Scriptures. Those pages, that paper, that ink is nothing; but the signs awaken something in us, into which flows the working of God's Spirit, and this spiritual working behind the signs—that is the miracle.[9]

This is not to say that Kuyper had a low regard for Holy Scripture. On the contrary! For him the Scriptures were the sole principium of theology, the sole source of the knowledge of God. He defended the infallibility of the Scriptures in opposition to the popular view of the so-called ethical theologians, who maintained that there were errors in Scripture.[10] In opposition to the ethical theologians, who said that the Word of God is *in* the Scripture, Kuyper maintained the principle that the Scripture *is* the Word of God. For Kuyper, the written Word was the clearest and highest expression of human consciousness. The Scripture thus brings us the Word of God as it has gone through and been ripened in human consciousness. The Scripture represents the highest form of revelation.[11]

Yet even in his later development, Kuyper consistently accents man as the subject and the direct work of the Holy Spirit in the heart of man. Scripture has only an auxiliary function in passing on revelation. Scripture is a living organism that orders itself. It has restoring power. However, it is a medium of grace and a tool for the Spirit. It is there because of sin, but we are moving ahead to the day when it will not be necessary anymore. Kuyper also said that the Bible is only an aid that works in an auxiliary way.[12] The real work of renewal, and the birth of the new life, is given to man without the Word, through the immediate working of the Holy Spirit, by which mankind is segregated into two parts: the church and the world, believers and unbelievers.

In this connection Kuyper made a distinction between *being* and *consciousness* in man, a distinction that plays a dominant role in all his thinking. With regard to the former, the work of the Holy Spirit is immediate. The seed of regeneration is planted directly by the Holy Spirit. With regard to the latter term, consciousness, the mediacy of revelation and Scripture is necessary in the post-Fall situation. The role of the Word of God and its proclamation is to bring the elect to the consciousness of His salvation.[13] Ultimately, both Scripture and revelation will not be needed when all is restored and the eternal Word is fully reflected in a renewed mankind.

In this situation Klaas Schilder began his work. His early writings were dominated by a thorough critique of dialectical theology.[14] He agreed with the dialectical theologians on one point: the absolute transcendence of God. He was even happy that these things were being said in Germany, for it was definitely necessary that they be voiced and heard. Schilder agreed that there is a great qualitative difference between God and man. He quoted Ecclesiastes 5:7 ("God is in heaven and you are on the earth, therefore let your words be few"), holding that this was a text opposing the arrogance of man before God. But, said Schilder, this is only half of the truth. God has come down to man. He is transcendent (above the world), but He is immanent (in the world) at the same time. He reveals Himself in acts, and at the same time He has made His revelation permanent by having it placed in writing. There is the act of revelation; there is also its abiding content.

How can we know the God who is exalted in majesty, beyond the power and strength of any man on the earth? Schilder answers that we can know Him because of His condescension in the covenant. This means that God bends down to us and approaches us in our state, and on our level. We also know Him because of His accommodation. Not only does He condescend to man's level in order to make Himself plain to man, but He also adapts all His words to man's level in order that they can be understood by man on his level. Never does He compromise with sin or sinful thought patterns. But His speech meshes in with man's brokenness in such a way that man can appropriate it. God has veiled His majesty, and He explains Himself in attributes shared by humankind in order that people will be able to understand Him.[15]

Schilder developed these themes on revelation in the context of the doctrine of the covenant. God condescends to man in the initiative of the covenant. In the framework of the covenant He opens His heart to man. We learn about His love, His wrath, His longsuffering, His patience, His vexation, His loyalty and faithfulness, and so on. In fact, the Bible has intimate passages. At one point, Moses sees the back of the Lord (Ex. 33:23). The Bible speaks about His mighty hand and His outstretched arm, His sense of smell, His anger, and so on. In every way the heart of God is disclosed. All this, for Schilder, is the language of accommodation. It is language not really suited to God and not exactly fitting for Him but chosen by Him in order to make Himself clear and plain to us.[16]

This principle of accommodation was not new but originated with Calvin.[17] It was Calvin who, more than any other before him, made use of this principle in his hermeneutics and his exegesis. It is found throughout his commentaries, and especially in those places where human qualities are attributed to God.[18]

With the idea of accommodation neither Calvin nor Schilder denied that the illumination of the Holy Spirit was necessary in order to understand properly the Word of God. But for Schilder, following Calvin, the tool of the Spirit—Holy Scripture—is no mean matter! The majesty of God is reflected in the text, which evinces such clarity that even the blind are able to follow and understand it. With this tool Schilder was able to answer the claims of dialectical theology and at the same time maintain the intrinsic majesty and transcendence of God. Barth said that God is essentially unknowable. He belongs to His sphere, we have our sphere, and these are two essentially different spheres. They never come together, and they are divided by a great chasm, a line of death. The line of death is like a tangent between two circles. In fact, these circles touch at only one point, and that point is Jesus Christ.[19] The reason they touch there is that He has overcome the power of death and so is able to cross the line of death. In Him God shatters all human knowledge, and in Him He gives the new knowledge of his grace.

Schilder responded to this speculative thinking by borrowing a term from article 13 of the Belgic Confession that also occurs frequently in Calvin, the term *limits* or *boundaries*. God has not set a "death line" between us and Him. He has set a limit, a boundary, beyond which we may not go. But He allows His revelation to enter history. In this way, He also steadily moves the limits back in proportion to the measure in which revelation progresses. With the Fall the limits shrank severely, but in Christ these are pushed back to their original place, and in fact they are expanded in the course of history as God commits His revelation to writing in Scripture. So there is not a line of death, but a boundary, the limits of which God sets according to His will.[20]

This was a forceful response to dialectical theology. In fact, it had a two-edged quality. It not only dealt a major blow to the claims of dialectical theology, but it also exposed many weaknesses in the Kuyperian view of revelation. For Schilder placed renewed emphasis upon God's great work with His Word. He also made a renewed plea for the priority and clarity of that Word in Scripture. The Word is God-breathed! All this is reflected in the principle of accommodation or adaptation to the level of man.

When Schilder began to bring some of these criticisms forward, a number of his contemporaries did not appreciate his criticism of Kuyper. They held on to Kuyper's view of revelation with its accent on the Spirit's inward work and its corollary, presumptive regeneration. In both views of Kuyper the underlying principle is the same: the direct work of God in the heart of the believer.[21] Hence, one must assume the child of the believer to be regenerated until the opposite should appear. Should the child not believe at maturity, his or her baptism has little or no significance. Baptism really only means something for the elect! In the renewed stress on the clear promise of Scripture, Schilder and others with him came into conflict with the bastion of traditional Kuyperianism. The conflict with Kuyperianism appeared rather unexpectedly, arising as it did out of the conflict with Barthianism. But once the conflict appeared, it pressed forward with rapid strides, affecting all areas of doctrine and life.[22]

As the conflict sharpened, the worst possible scenario began to unfold. Schilder was found to be heretical in his views, and together with many others who denied presumptive regeneration, he was deposed from office. But when all the pieces fell into place after the "big bang" of the Liberation, this was the result: some of the staunch defenders of Kuyperianism were found to be bedfellows with those who were leading figures in dialectical theology. This in itself is not difficult to understand; like attracts like. And some representatives of both streams of thought found each other on the essential subjectivist starting point that characterized both classic Kuyperianism and dialectical theology![23]

We now turn to the relevance of this battle concerning revelation for today. This may not readily be apparent, since dialectical theology did something of a turnabout in its later period. Barth began to stress the condescension of God, and then he began to accent what he called the *humanity* of God. For Barth this meant that there was no God besides the one who speaks in the avenues laid down in Scripture. God's revelation event has a natural, bodily, outward, and visible component. This also has implications for the description of God's being. Here Barth rejected the classic view of accommodation as defended by Calvin and Schilder and insisted on taking the Old Testament texts at face value, holding that God in His way really has the physical organs and feelings attributed to Him.[24]

This was just the beginning. There followed a stream of theological movements that not only reinstated history to a respectable level, but also put God back into history—so much so that men began to give Him a human and thoroughly historical, time-conditioned form! We cannot go into detail here. Suffice it to say that this became the general trend in postwar European and American theological thinking.[25]

This line was followed by H. M. Kuitert, a student of G. C. Berkouwer. He holds that there is only one God and that He is exactly as He is described in the Old Testament. He is "Hebreomorphic," that is, He has no eternal essence apart from the description of His words and deeds in the Old Testament.[26] He is Israel's Partner or Ally. Yet these Old Testament writings are only texts that direct one to the encounter with God. Later Kuitert says that the biblical texts are only layers of tradition that reflect an encounter with the divine and so point the way to God. The Bible is open-ended! We need the Bible with its traditions in order to make God's Word come alive today. But the Bible is certainly not a closed canon, nor is it divinely inspired. Through listening to the texts and hearing them in our situation over and over again, we move forward to a greater disclosure of God. Essentially, He is the object of our search. Essentially, He is unknown to us![27]

The character of the turnabout in dialectical theology is clear. In simple terms, where the early dialectical theology brought Scripture down to a human level, the later dialectical theology and many complementary and supplementary movements took the next step: to bring God down to a human level. At the same time, they make Him all that much more unknowable by implying that the full disclosure of God is something reserved for the future and that what people share today are only partial manifestations of His presence.

The central issue here is one's view of revelation. The school of Berkouwer, the direct inheritors and original defenders of Kuyperianism, hold the Bible to be a time-bound book. As such it includes all the limitations of the thought world of its authors. The human factor, according to Berkouwer a factor much too neglected, is an essential element in the explanation of the text. Fundamentally, Berkouwer and his followers hold that the Bible must be seen as a book of its time and that it is only in the faith recognition of its limitations that it really speaks to the believer. The real focus must not be on the Bible's form, but on its content.[28]

Against this background one can see the abiding relevance of the work of Dr. K. Schilder. At a crucial juncture in the history of theology and philosophy he sought to uphold the correct view of Scripture and the world that it describes, including, above all, the God whom it describes. Today we do him the greatest honor when in our situation we continue to uphold Scripture in a world that increasingly denies the presence of the authoritative voice of God in its midst. This does not ask for thoughtless repetition of what Schilder said, but a sympathetic-critical review of his arguments and a sympathetic-critical application of those arguments to today's theological situation. We ought not to glorify men, but to thank God for the instruments that He has used to uphold His Word. That is the thrust of the text with which we began; ending with it will, I hope, confirm my point: "Remember your leaders, those who spoke to you the *Word of God;* consider the outcome of their life, and imitate their faith."

Notes

1. K. Schilder, *Zur Begriffsgeschichte des "Paradoxon," mit besonderer Berücksichtigung Calvins und des nach-Kierkegaardschen "Paradoxon"* (Kampen: Kok, 1933).

2. K. Schilder, "Schrift en Schriftbeschouwing" (Scripture and the View of Scripture), *De Reformatie* 12, no. 26 (1932): 202.

3. K. Barth, *Church Dogmatics,* trans. G. W. Bromiley (Edinburgh: T. & T. Clark, 1936), vol. 1, pt. 1, 305–9. On Barth's view of revelation, see H. Zahrnt, *The Question of God. Protestant Theology in the Twentieth Century,* trans. R. A. Wilson (New York: Harcourt, Brace and World, 1969).

4. A. Kuyper, *Dictaten Dogmatiek* (Kampen: Kok, n.d.), 1:36. It should be noted that Kuyper's Lectures on Dogmatics are students' excerpts of what Kuyper said in his lectures, which, as Kuyper wrote, do not all have equal value, as "one finds some of very good quality, others of a doubtful quality, and also others of inferior quality" (p. iii).

5. A. Kuyper, *Principles of Sacred Theology,* trans. B. B. Warfield (Grand Rapids: Eerdmans, 1954), 366, 389.

6. C. Trimp, "Het Patroon van het Calvinisme," *De Dienst van de Mondige Kerk* (Goes: Oosterbaan & Le Cointre, 1971), 9–48, esp. pp. 11, 18.

7. Kuyper, *Dictaten Dogmatiek,* 2:64, 71, 91.

8. A. Kuyper, *Encyclopaedie der Heilige Godgeleerdheid* (Kampen: Kok, 1909), 112.

9. Kuyper, *Dictaten Dogmatiek,* 2:98.

10. The *ethical movement* is the name given to that group of theologians in the Netherlands of the nineteenth century that grew out of the school of the Swiss theologian Alexander Vinet (1797–1847). The leading figure in this school was Daniël Chantepie de la Saussaye (1818–74). This school had an affinity for the thought of F. L. Schleiermacher in Germany in that it wanted to build theology and dogma on the basis of the experience of the congregation. Although initially influenced by this movement, Kuyper went on to oppose it by a return to the Scriptures as God's Word. See, for example, his address on becoming a rector, *De Hedendaagsche Schriftcritiek in hare Bedenkelijke Strekking voor de Gemeenten des Levenden Gods* (The Present-Day Bible Criticism in Its Questionable Tenor for the Congregations of the Living God) (Amsterdam: J. H. Kruyt, 1881). In this address Kuyper uses the image of the diamond and light for the relation between the Spirit and the Scripture and rejects the view that there is a supernatural power in Scripture itself. Kuyper incorrectly attributes this view strictly to the Lutherans, and not to Calvin. Calvin also maintained that Scripture exudes a divine energy (*vis*) in itself; see S. Greijdanus, "Karakter van het Testimonium Spiritus Sancti volgens Calvijn," *Gereformeerd Theologisch Tijdschrift* 14, no. 12 (1913): 540.

11. Kuyper's break with the ethical theologians occurred as early as 1870, when he was a minister in Amsterdam. He was invited to write an introduction to a

volume of collected articles dealing with the history of revelation. The authors were selected from the various camps of Protestantism in Holland. When the introduction was read by those who had committed themselves to the project, five of them withdrew, expressing their disagreement with Kuyper's standpoint. In order to salvage his project, the publisher sought another minister to introduce the volume. Kuyper's draft introduction was later published as a separate brochure, *De Schrift, het Woord Gods* (Scripture, the Word of God) (Tiel: H. C. A. Campagne, 1870).

12. Kuyper, *Principles of Sacred Theology,* 361. See also *De Schrift, het Woord Gods,* 46.

13. For Kuyper on regeneration and baptism, see R. J. Dam et al., *Rondom 1905: een Historische Schets* (About 1905: An Historical Outline) (Terneuzen: Littooij, n.d.), 7.

14. See, for example, K. Schilder, *Bij Dichters en Schriftgeleerden* (Among Poets and Scribes) (Amsterdam: Holland, 1927), and K. Schilder, Tusschen *"Ja" en "Neen"* (Between Yes and No) (Kampen: Kok, 1929).

15. K. Schilder, *Heidelbergsche Catechismus,* 4 vols. (Goes: Oosterbaan & Le Cointre, 1947–51), 2:105.

16. Ibid., 4:99, 104–6.

17. Actually, Calvin took it over from Chrysostom and other church fathers; but for his use of the term Schilder is indebted strictly to Calvin.

18. For examples from Calvin, see J. De Jong, *Accommodatio Dei—A Theme in K. Schilder's Theology of Revelation* (Kampen: Mondiss, 1990), 239–66.

19. A. D. R. Polman, *Barth.* Modern Thinkers Series (Philadelphia: Presbyterian and Reformed, 1968), 13.

20. Schilder, *Zur Begriffsgeschichte des "Paradoxon,"* 448–62.

21. It would lead us too far afield to work this out. Here the reader is referred to J. Kamphuis, *An Everlasting Covenant,* trans. G. van Rongen (Launceston, Australia: Publication Organization of the Free Reformed Churches, 1985), 23–27.

22. In "Vernieuwing en conflict in de jaren dertig" (Renewal and conflict in the thirties) in D. Deddens and M. te Velde, eds., *Vrijmaking—Wederkeer. Vijftig jaar Vrijmaking in beeld gebracht 1944–1994* (Liberation—Return. A Picture of Fifty Years Liberation 1944–1994) (Barneveld, the Netherlands: De Vuurbaak, 1994), 28, M. te Velde says that Schilder found the scholastic structures of Kuyperian theology to be inadequate to deal with the problems and heresies arising in his generation.

23. It is remarkable that Kuyper also used the expression (later typical of Barth) that Scripture is a *witness* to God's revelation (Kuyper, *Principles of Sacred Theology,* 360). Of course, Kuyper's use of this term should not be construed as Barthian!

24. Barth, *Church Dogmatics,* vol. 2, pt. 1, 265. Barth rejects the accommodation principle specifically as it was defended by the Reformed theologian A. Polanus, *Syntagma Theologiae Christianae* (1609); see *Church Dogmatics,* vol. 2, pt. 1, 266.

25. A good example of—and at the same time a good introduction to—this way of thinking can be found in H. M. Kuitert, *The Reality of Faith: A Way Between Protestant Orthodoxy and Existentialist Theology,* trans. L. B. Smedes (Grand Rapids: Eerdmans, 1968).

26. H. M. Kuitert, *De Mensvormigheid Gods. Een dogmatisch–hermeneutische Studie over de Anthropomorfismen van de Heilige Schrift* (The Anthropomorphic Nature of God: A Dogmatic-hermeneutic Study About the Anthropomorphisms of Holy Scripture) (Kampen: Kok, 1862), 277.

27. Cf. H. M. Kuitert, *Wat Heet Geloven? Structuur en Herkomst van de Christelijke Geloofsuitspraken* (What Is Believing? Structure and Origin of the Christian Pronouncements of Faith) (Baarn: Ten Have, 1977).

28. G. C. Berkouwer, *De Heilige Schrift* (Kampen: Kok, 1967), 2:58–61, 93–100.

CONTRIBUTORS

J. M. Batteau was born in 1946 in the United States. He studied theology at Westminster Theological Seminary, at the Free University in Amsterdam, and at the Theological University of the (Liberated) Reformed Churches in the Netherlands, where he earned the doctorandus in theology degree. After ordination in the (Liberated) Reformed Church at Meppel (1979), he was sent out as missionary professor and taught dogmatology at the Theological Seminary of the Presbyterian Church (Kosin) at Pusan, South Korea, from 1980 to 1988. After his return to the Netherlands, he served as minister of the Reformed Church at Zaandam (1988–94), and, since 1994, the (Liberated) Reformed Church at Wageningen.

J. De Jong was born in 1949 in Canada. He studied theology at the Theological College of the Canadian Reformed Churches in Hamilton, Ontario. He continued his studies at the Theological University in Kampen. He served the Canadian Reformed churches at London (1978–83) and Burlington-South (1983–90). In 1990, he earned his doctor's degree with a dissertation *Accomodatio Dei. A Theme in K. Schilder's Theology of Revelation.* Since 1990 he has taught ecclesiology and diaconiology at the Theological College of the Canadian Reformed Churches in Hamilton.

J. Faber was born in 1924 in the Netherlands. He studied theology at the Theological Seminary of the (undivided) Reformed Churches and after 1944 at the University of the (Liberated) Reformed Churches at Kampen, the Netherlands. He was a minister in Deventer (1952–58) and Schiebroek-Hillegersberg-Centrum (Rotterdam) (1958–69). In 1969 he earned his doctor's degree with a dissertation *Vestigium Ecclesiae: De Doop als 'spoor der kerk' (Cyprianus, Optatus, Augustinus)* (Baptism as "Vestige of the Church"). In the same year, Dr. Faber moved to Canada to serve as Professor of Dogmatology and Principal at the newly established Theological College of the Canadian Reformed Churches at Hamilton, Ontario. He retired in 1990.

J. Geertsema was born in 1935 in the Netherlands. He studied at the Theological University of the (Liberated) Reformed Churches at Kampen, the Netherlands. He served the (Liberated) Reformed churches at Kantens (1963–67), and at Opende and Surhuisterveen (1967–71), the Netherlands, and the Canadian Reformed Churches at Carman, Manitoba (1971–76), Chatham, Ontario (1976–81), and Surrey, British Columbia (1981–86). Since 1986 he has taught New Testament at the Theological College of the Canadian Reformed Churches at Hamilton, Ontario. In 1991, he obtained the degree of Master of Theology at Wycliffe College and the Toronto School of Theology.

N. H. Gootjes was born in 1948 in the Netherlands. After his study at the Theological University of the (Liberated) Reformed Churches at Kampen, the Netherlands, he became minister of the Reformed Church at Leiden (1976) and was called as missionary Professor of New Testament Greek and Dogmatics from 1980 to 1989 at the Theological Seminary of the Presbyterian Church (Kosin) at Pusan, South Korea. Dr. Gootjes obtained his doctor's degree with a dissertation on *De Geestelijkheid van God* (The Spirituality of God). Succeeding Dr. J. Faber, Dr. Gootjes has since 1989 been Professor of Dogmatology at the Theological College of the Canadian Reformed Churches at Hamilton.

J. Kamphuis was born in 1921 in the Netherlands. He studied at the Theological Seminary of the (undivided) Reformed Churches and after

1944 at the Theological University of the (Liberated) Reformed Churches at Kampen, the Netherlands. He served the Reformed Churches (Liberated) at Ferwerd and Hallum (1948–51), Bunschoten-Spakenburg (1951–55), and Rotterdam-Delfshaven (1955–59). In 1959, he was appointed Professor of Ecclesiology at the Theological University of the Reformed Churches (Liberated) in Kampen. In 1979 the Synod of these churches appointed him Professor of Dogmatology at the same university. Since 1987 Professor Kamphuis has been retired.

S. A. Strauss was born in 1946 in South Africa. He studied theology at the University of Stellenbosch, and became minister of the Nederduitse Gereformeerde Kerk in 1974. After having spent a year in Kampen, the Netherlands in 1981, doing research, he earned his doctor's degree at the University of Pretoria in 1982 with a dissertation entitled *Alles of Niks. K. Schilder oor die verbond* (All or Nothing: K. Schilder About the Covenant). Since 1984, Dr. Strauss has been Professor of Dogmatology at the University of Bloemfontein, in the Orange Free State.

INDEX OF SCRIPTURE

INDEX OF NAMES

INDEX OF SUBJECTS